Student Workbook

GLOBE FEARON

American History

The following people have contributed to the development of this product:

Art & Design: Kathleen Ellison, Jim O'Shea, Eileen Peters, Angel Weyant
Editorial: Elaine Fay, Alisa Loftus, Colleen Maguire, Jane Petlinski
Manufacturing: Nathan Kinney
Marketing: Katie Erezuma
Production: Travis Bailey, Irene Belinsky, Karen Edmonds, Phyllis Rosinsky, Cindy Talocci
Publishing Operations: Kate Matracia, Karen McCollum

ISBN 0-130-23813-9

Printed in the United States of America
  2 3 4 5 6 7 8 9 10   06 05 04 03 02

Globe Fearon
Pearson Learning Group

1-800-321-3106
www.pearsonlearning.com

CONTENTS

Geography Handbook

A. Each of the following descriptions relates to the five themes of geography: *location, place, region, movement,* **or** *human interaction.* **Write the correct term on the line below each description.**

1. The Pilgrims came to North America seeking religious freedom.

   _____

2. Some farmers cut down trees to clear the land for their crops.

   _____

3. New Orleans, Louisiana, and Houston, Texas, are both located at a latitude of approximately 30° N.

   _____

4. The northern part of Mexico is dry, and most of its land is flat.

   _____

5. Many Americans made their way to California in search of gold.

   _____

6. Dust storms often sweep the level, almost treeless prairies of North Dakota.

   _____

7. The southern part of the United States has a climate that is warmer than the northern part.

   _____

8. The Trans-Alaska Pipeline was built to transport oil across 800 miles of Alaska.

   _____

B. Write a paragraph describing ways in which people in your region interact with their environment. Write your paragraph on a separate sheet of paper.

Geography Handbook

Use the map to answer the following questions.

The Midwest and the Great Plains Region

CANADA

North Dakota
Grand Forks
Bismarck ★   Fargo •
Duluth •
Minnesota
Lake Superior

South Dakota
Rapid City •   Pierre ★   Missouri River   Sioux Falls •
Minneapolis •   St. Paul ★
Green Bay •
Wisconsin
Mississippi River
Lake Michigan   Michigan   Lake Huron
Grand Rapids •
Milwaukee •   Detroit •
Madison ★   Lansing ★
Lake Erie

Nebraska
Grand Island •   Omaha •
Lincoln ★
Sioux City •
Iowa
Cedar Rapids •   Des Moines ★
Rockford •
Chicago •
Gary •   Fort Wayne •   Cleveland •

Kansas
Topeka ★   Lawrence •
Kansas City •
Missouri
Jefferson City ★
Springfield •
Illinois
St. Louis •
Indiana
Indianapolis ★
Ohio
Columbus ★
Cincinnati •
Ohio River

Wichita •
Arkansas River

N W E S

★ State capitals
• Major cities

0   100   200 mi
0   100   200 km

1. Which symbol is used to show state capitals on this map?

_____

2. What is the capital of Nebraska?

_____

3. Which states border Iowa to the west?

_____

4. If you were to travel from South Dakota to Michigan, would you be moving north, south, east, or west?

_____

Geography Handbook

Use the map to answer the following questions.

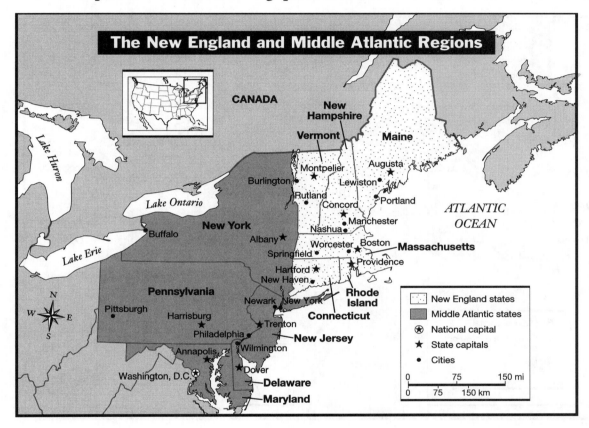

The New England and Middle Atlantic Regions

CANADA

Lake Huron

Lake Ontario

Lake Erie

Buffalo •

New York

Albany ★

New Hampshire

Vermont

Maine

Montpelier ★

Burlington •

Augusta ★

Lewiston •

Rutland •

Portland •

Concord ★

Manchester •

Nashua •

Worcester •

Boston ★

Massachusetts

Springfield •

Providence •

Hartford ★

New Haven •

Rhode Island

Pennsylvania

Pittsburgh •

Harrisburg ★

Newark • New York •

Trenton ★

Connecticut

New Jersey

Philadelphia •

Wilmington •

Annapolis ★

Washington, D.C. ⊛

Dover ★

Delaware

Maryland

ATLANTIC OCEAN

N W E S

Legend:
- New England states
- Middle Atlantic states
- ⊛ National capital
- ★ State capitals
- • Cities

0   75   150 mi
0   75   150 km

1. What is the capital of Connecticut?

_____

2. Which states are part of the New England region?

_____

3. What is the distance between Washington, D.C., and Wilmington, Delaware?

_____

4. If you were to travel from Albany, New York, to Trenton, New Jersey, would you be moving north, south, east, or west?

_____

© Pearson Education, Inc. Copying strictly prohibited.

Geography Handbook   **7**

Geography Handbook

Reading a Map

Use the map to answer the following questions.

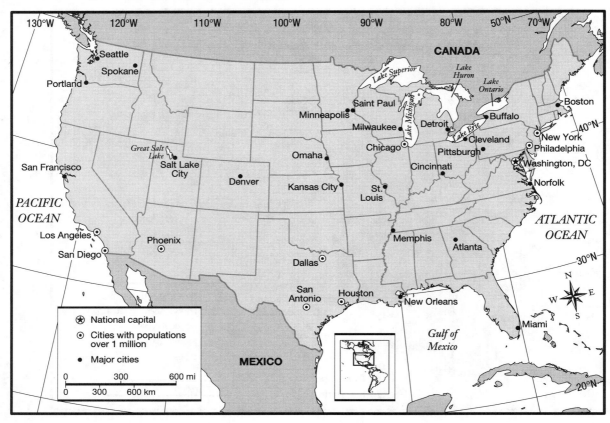

1. Which symbol is used to show major cities on this map?

_____

2. Which cities on this map have populations of more than one million?

_____

3. If you were to travel from Chicago to San Francisco, would you be moving north, south, east, or west?

_____

4. Which two cities on this map are closest to Canada?

_____

Geography Handbook

Using Latitude

Use the map to answer the following questions.

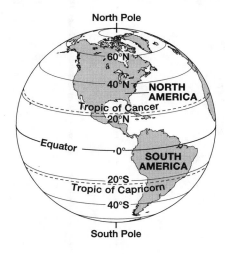

North Pole

60°N

40°N

NORTH AMERICA

Tropic of Cancer

20°N

Equator — 0°

SOUTH AMERICA

20°S

Tropic of Capricorn

40°S

South Pole

1. What unit of measurement is used to identify lines of latitude?

_____

2. What is the latitude at the equator?

_____

3. North America and South America are continents. Which continent does the equator pass through?

_____

4. The Southern Hemisphere is the half of the globe that lies south of the equator. Which continent shown on the map is in the Southern Hemisphere?

_____

5. Which continent does the Tropic of Capricorn pass through?

_____

Geography Handbook

Using Longitude

Use the map to answer the following questions.

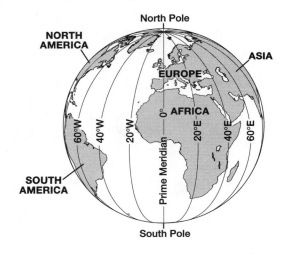

1. Which unit of measurement is used to identify lines of longitude?

_____

2. What is the longitude at the prime meridian?

_____

3. Which continents does the prime meridian pass through?

_____

4. The Western Hemisphere is the half of the globe that lies west of the prime meridian. Which continents shown on the map are in the Western Hemisphere?

_____

5. The Eastern Hemisphere is the half of the globe that lies east of the prime meridian. Which continents shown on the map are in the Eastern Hemisphere?

_____

Geography Handbook

Using Latitude and Longitude

Use the map to answer the following questions.

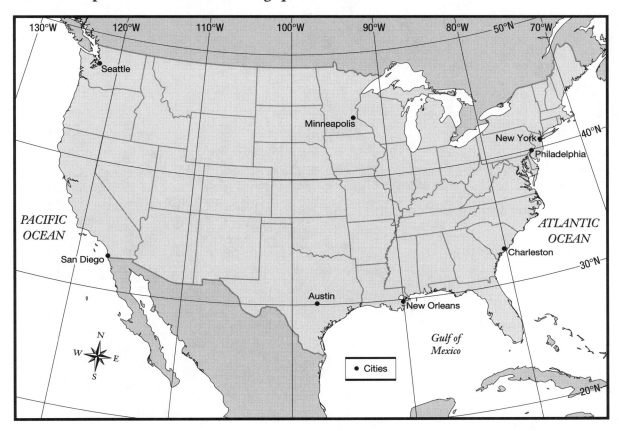

1. Which two cities are closest to 120°W?

_____

2. What is the approximate latitude and longitude of Minneapolis?

_____

3. Which two cities are closest to 30°N?

_____

4. What is the approximate latitude and longitude of Charleston?

_____

Geography Handbook

Map Projections

Use the maps to answer the following questions.

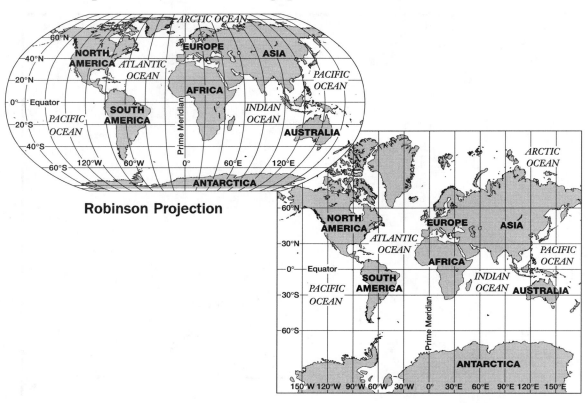

Robinson Projection

Mercator Projection

1. What does a flat map allow you to do?

_____

2. Which map projection shows curved lines of latitude and longitude?

_____

3. Which map projection shows straight lines of latitude and longitude?

_____

4. Which map projection shows the true shapes of landmasses, but distorts their sizes?

_____

Complete the chart below. Give two details for each main idea.
The first one is done for you.

Main Idea	Details
A. Hunters in search of food were the first people to live in the Americas.	1. *Hunters followed herds of animals.* 2.
B. Different groups of Native Americans used the resources available in their region.	3. 4.
C. Native American men and women both contributed to their community.	5. 6.

Critical Thinking

Draw Conclusions
Why is it important to know how people lived in the past?
Write your answer on a separate sheet of paper.

Complete each sentence with a term from the box.

Toltec	Anasazi	Maya	Adena-Hopewell
Olmecs	Aztecs	Mississippian	

1. The _____ built a huge empire in Mexico, whose capital city was Tenochtitlán.

2. The people of the _____ civilization lived in large towns or trading centers.

3. The _____ built apartment-like structures of stone and sun-dried clay.

4. The _____ Empire was based on warfare and at its height extended from the Gulf Coast into Central America.

5. The burial mounds of the _____ people contain artifacts that tell us they traded with groups in the Rocky Mountains.

6. The _____, who were among the first people to thrive on Mexico's Gulf Coast, invented calendars and writing systems.

7. The _____ used their knowledge of the stars to keep track of planting and harvest cycles.

Critical Thinking

Evaluate
Write a journal entry describing what life must have been like in the ancient empire of the Incas. Write your journal entry on a separate sheet of paper.

Section III. Native Americans

Write *true* or *false* on the line below each sentence. If the sentence is false, rewrite it to make it true. Use a separate sheet of paper if you need more space.

1. The Pueblos planted crops in ditches where rainwater collected.

   _____

2. After cutting and burning trees, the Eskimos planted crops in the cleared land.

   _____

3. People along the Pacific Coast traded dried salmon with other Native Americans for tools and clothing.

   _____

4. Native Americans of the Great Plains moved often to follow caribou herds.

   _____

5. The Anasazi were one of the earliest Native American groups to inhabit the Southwest.

   _____

6. Some Inuit groups used sleds pulled by a person or a dog team to carry heavy loads over snow and ice.

   _____

7. Groups such as the Paiutes and Shoshones lived in the Great Basin.

   _____

Critical Thinking

Draw Conclusions

Changes in landscape throughout North America forced Native Americans to adapt to their surroundings for survival. Which group do you think had the most difficult time adapting? Explain. Write your answer on a separate sheet of paper.

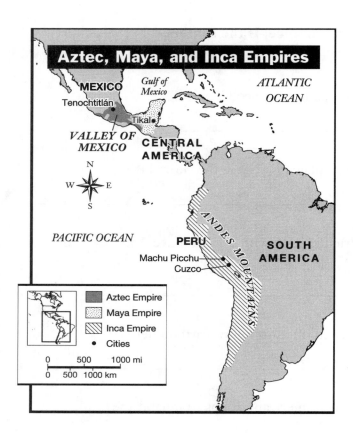

Use the map to answer the following questions.

1. Where was the Aztec Empire located?

_____

2. Where was the Inca Empire located?

_____

3. Which empires are bordered by the Gulf of Mexico?

_____

4. What cities are shown on the map?

_____

2 Section I. West African Trading Kingdoms

Write *true* or *false* on the line below each sentence. If the sentence is false, rewrite it to make it true. Use a separate sheet of paper if you need more space.

1. The rulers of Songhai made Timbuktu into a famous center of learning.

_____

2. Before 1400, Africans considered gold to have a far greater value than salt.

_____

3. Most West Africans living outside of trading centers depended on hunting for food.

_____

4. Savannas are good farming areas that lie north and south of Africa's rain forests.

_____

5. Slavery was unknown in Africa before the arrival of the Europeans.

_____

6. The trading kingdoms of Ghana, Mali, and Songhai were all located on the northern edge of the Sahara.

_____

7. Much of North Africa was ruled by Muslims between 1000 and 1450.

_____

8. The northern and southern parts of Africa contain deserts.

_____

Critical Thinking

Synthesize Information
You are a merchant in West Africa. Explain how you might transport your products to people in Europe. Write your answer on a separate sheet of paper.

Section II. Early European Expeditions

Complete each sentence with a term from the box.

Holy Land	Silk Road	Europe	Portugal
Africa	Madeira Islands	Mediterranean Sea	

1. In the 1400s, Portuguese settlers established sugar plantations on the

_____.

2. The Crusades led to trade between Muslim people and the people of

_____.

3. The Italians controlled the trade routes on the _____.

4. The region of land surrounding the city of Jerusalem was known as the

_____.

5. Prince Henry wanted _____ to control trade with Asia.

6. The _____ was an overland route that extended from

Europe to eastern Asia.

7. In 1498, Vasco da Gama sailed around _____ to India, giving

Portugal an advantage in the competition for trade among European nations.

Critical Thinking

Recognize Relationships
How did the Crusades ultimately lead to the establishment of trade routes and the discovery and exploration of new lands? Write your answer on a separate sheet of paper.

2 Section III. Major Voyages to the Americas

Match each item with its description. Write the correct letter on the line.

_____ **1.** Portuguese explorer who claimed land on the shore of present-day Brazil for Portugal

_____ **2.** Portugal's main rival in overseas exploration

_____ **3.** sailors from Scandinavia who came to the shores of North America under the command of Leif Ericson

_____ **4.** explorer who offered to sail for Queen Isabella and King Ferdinand if they would provide ships and crews

_____ **5.** the island that Columbus landed on and thought was Asia

_____ **6.** French explorer who sailed from France to present-day South Carolina

_____ **7.** Native Americans whom Columbus encountered on San Salvador island

_____ **8.** the Caribbean island that Columbus returned to in 1493 to make a Spanish colony

_____ **9.** explorer who sailed for France and who tried to establish a settlement along the St. Lawrence River

_____ **10.** explorer who sailed for Spain and became the first to sail completely around the world

a. Norsemen

b. Christopher Columbus

c. San Salvador

d. Spain

e. Pedro Cabral

f. Giovanni da Verrazano

g. Jacques Cartier

h. Hispaniola

i. Táino

j. Ferdinand Magellan

Critical Thinking

Draw Conclusions
What do you think the Native Americans thought as they watched a Viking ship come toward shore? Do you think they were excited or scared? Explain. Write your answer on a separate sheet of paper.

2 Using a Chart

Some Early Portuguese and Spanish Explorations, 1488–1522				
EXPLORER	**COUNTRY REPRESENTED**	**YEAR**	**GOAL**	**ACCOMPLISHMENT**
Bartolomeu Dias	Portugal	1487–1488	To find southern tip of Africa	Sailed around southern Africa into Indian Ocean
Christopher Columbus	Spain	1492–1504 (4 voyages)	To find western route to Asia	Explored West Indies and Central and South America
Vasco da Gama	Portugal	1497–1498	To sail around Africa to eastern Asia	Reached India
Vasco Núñez de Balboa	Spain	1513	To find gold	Crossed Isthmus of Panama and saw Pacific Ocean
Ferdinand Magellan	Spain	1519–1522	To find western route to Asia	First expedition to sail around the world

Use the chart to answer the following questions.

1. Which explorer sailed around Africa and reached India?

_____

2. Which two explorers sailed for Portugal?

_____

3. Which explorer made four voyages over twelve years?

_____

4. Which two explorers were at sea in 1497?

_____

5. What was the goal of Vasco Núñez de Balboa in 1513?

_____

A. Choose the answer that best completes each of the following sentences. Circle the letter of the correct answer.

1. Hernándo Cortés went to the east coast of the Gulf of Mexico to find

   a. gold.

   b. spices.

   c. the Fountain of Youth.

   d. enslaved people.

2. Spaniards came to the Americas to

   a. expand the Spanish Empire.

   b. search for gold.

   c. spread the Catholic faith.

   d. all of the above

3. Under Spanish rule, many Native Americans were

   a. taught to read and write.

   b. overworked and died from disease.

   c. given the rights of a Spanish citizen.

   d. allowed to travel to Spain.

4. Francisco Coronado explored the

   a. present-day American Southwest.

   b. present-day New England coast.

   c. present-day coast of South America.

   d. mountains of Peru.

B. Answer each question on the lines below.

5. What was the Columbian Exchange?

   _____

6. What did Ponce de León hope to find when he left Puerto Rico in 1513?

   _____

7. What was the encomienda system?

   _____

Critical Thinking

Synthesize Information

Write about one of the explorers you read about. What did he find when he came to the Americas? Describe the things he saw, heard, and touched. Write your answer on a separate sheet of paper.

Match each item with its description. Write the correct letter on the line.

_____ 1. English explorer who was hired by Dutch merchants from the Netherlands to find a Northwest Passage

a. Samuel de Champlain

_____ 2. English explorer who was given a charter by Queen Elizabeth of England to start a colony in North America

b. Robert de La Salle

_____ 3. a group of investors who share both risk and profit

c. Spanish Armada

_____ 4. the company that was given a charter to send settlers to the Atlantic Coast of North America

d. New Netherland

_____ 5. the first permanent English settlement in North America

e. joint-stock company

_____ 6. French explorer who founded Quebec in 1608

f. Jamestown

_____ 7. settlement led by John White where 117 colonists vanished

g. tobacco

_____ 8. French explorer who claimed the entire Mississippi River valley for France

h. Roanoke Island

_____ 9. Jamestown's most important cash crop

i. cash crop

_____ 10. a huge fleet of ships sent to conquer England in 1588

j. Virginia Company

_____ 11. colony that was founded by Dutch traders and covered the Hudson River valley

k. Henry Hudson

_____ 12. a crop that is grown to be sold rather than used by a farmer

l. Sir Walter Raleigh
.

Critical Thinking

Evaluate
Life in Jamestown was rather difficult in the colony's early years. How was the settlement improved under the leadership of John Smith? Write your answer on a separate sheet of paper.

Section III. Slavery in the Americas

Answer each question on the lines below.

1. How did West African society change after the slave trade with Portugal increased in the mid-1400s?

_____

2. What happened to enslaved men and women after they were sold to Portuguese traders?

_____

3. What were conditions like for enslaved Africans on slave ships?

_____

4. Why did Spaniards begin importing African slaves to sugar plantations on the Caribbean islands of Cuba and Hispaniola?

_____

5. Which European countries set up sugar colonies in the Caribbean and imported African slaves?

_____

6. When did Portuguese traders first take slaves from Africa?

_____

7. What was the original source of labor on the English sugar plantations in the Caribbean?

_____

Critical Thinking

Recognize Relationships
Explain why the slave trade became an important part of the economy in the Americas. Write your answer on a separate sheet of paper.

Africans to the Americas, 1451–1810	
DESTINATION	**NUMBER OF PEOPLE**
Brazil	2,501,400
English colonies	2,013,000
French colonies	1,600,200
Spanish colonies	945,600
Dutch colonies	500,000

Use the chart to answer the following questions.

1. To which destination did the least number of Africans go?

_____

2. To which destination did 945,600 Africans go?

_____

3. How many Africans were brought to Brazil?

_____

4. To which destination did 2,013,000 Africans go?

_____

5. How many Africans were brought to the French colonies?

_____

Section I. New England Colonies

Write the events in the box below in the order in which they occurred. The first one is done for you.

Colonists attack Pequot settlements along the Connecticut River.

Pilgrims sail from England to North America on the *Mayflower*.

Colonists defeat the Wampanoags in King Philip's War.

English merchants receive charter to start a fishing and lumbering colony.

Roger Williams founds the town of Providence.

Thomas Hooker and followers leave Boston.

Martin Luther protests the policies of the Catholic Church.

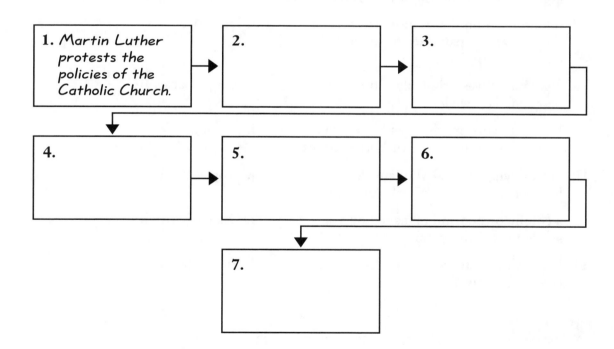

1. Martin Luther protests the policies of the Catholic Church.

2.

3.

4.

5.

6.

7.

Critical Thinking

Recognize Relationships

Why was the first winter in Plymouth so difficult for the colonists? How did life in North America finally improve? Write your answer on a separate sheet of paper.

Match each item with its description. Write the correct letter on the line.

_____ **1.** Dutch landowners in the colony of New Netherland

_____ **2.** colonists who grew only enough crops to meet their everyday needs

_____ **3.** the "City of Brotherly Love"

_____ **4.** owner of the colony of Pennsylvania

_____ **5.** colony that allowed people to practice all religions freely

_____ **6.** person who claimed the colony of New Netherland for the English in 1664

_____ **7.** religious group that refused to serve in the military or pay taxes to support the Church of England

_____ **8.** colony that was originally settled by people from Sweden

_____ **9.** Dutch governor who was forced to surrender to the Duke of York's forces

_____ **10.** person who granted William Penn a large area of land in North America

_____ **11.** a colony owned and managed by a single person or group

_____ **12.** French Protestants who settled in the colony of New York

a. Quakers

b. Huguenots

c. William Penn

d. Peter Stuyvesant

e. subsistence farmers

f. Pennsylvania

g. Delaware

h. King Charles II

i. patroons

j. proprietary colony

k. Duke of York

l. Philadelphia

Critical Thinking

Evaluate
How did the Duke of York's attitude toward acquiring land differ from William Penn's? Explain your position using facts from Section II. Write your answer on a separate sheet of paper.

Complete the chart below by writing two facts about each colony.
The first one is done for you.

Colony	Year Established	Facts
Virginia	1607	1. *Began with the English settlement of Jamestown* 2.
Maryland	1633	3. 4.
Carolina	1663	5. 6.
Georgia	1733	7. 8.

Critical Thinking

Evaluate
Create a timeline using the dates in Section III. Label
each date with an event that happened at that time.
Draw your timeline on a separate sheet of paper.

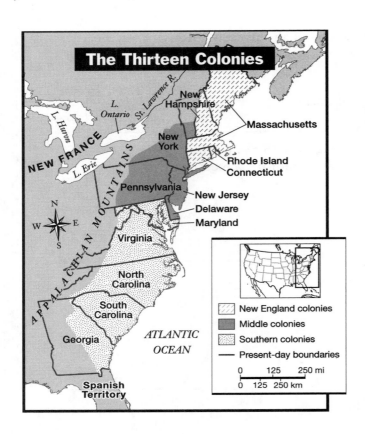

Use the map to answer the following questions.

1. Which colony is farthest south?

_____

2. Which colonies share a peninsula?

_____

3. How many colonies are Southern colonies?

_____

4. Which colonies border Connecticut?

_____

Section I. The Colonial Economy

Answer each question on the lines below.

1. What system was the English economy based on in the 1600s?

_____

2. Where did manufacturing in colonial towns take place?

_____

3. What were farms like in New England?

_____

4. What crops were grown in the Southern colonies?

_____

5. What action was taken by some of the merchants who did not agree with the Navigation Acts?

_____

6. What were the natural resources in New England?

_____

7. What industries were people in the Middle colonies involved in?

_____

8. Who made up the labor force on plantations in the Southern colonies?

_____

Critical Thinking

Recognize Relationships
How did the passage of the Navigation Acts cause conflict between England and the colonies? Write your answer on a separate sheet of paper.

5 Section II. Life in the Colonies

Choose the answer that best completes each of the following sentences. Circle the letter of the correct answer.

1. The Zenger trial marked
   a. the founding of the first college in the colonies.
   b. the beginning of the Enlightenment.
   c. a step toward freedom of the press in America.
   d. the beginning of the Great Awakening.

2. Many Enlightenment philosophers wanted to
   a. start a new religious movement.
   b. discover how the universe worked.
   c. work as apprentices.
   d. set up both primary and secondary schools in their towns.

3. Boys in the New England colonies
   a. were not expected to help with farm work.
   b. sometimes worked as apprentices.
   c. were not allowed to go to school.
   d. were not strictly supervised.

4. Colonial women
   a. had the same rights as men.
   b. could vote and serve on juries.
   c. were able to keep control of their property once they were married.
   d. did not have many legal rights.

5. In colonial society, newspapers
   a. printed only news from Europe.
   b. were not important to colonists.
   c. were strictly controlled by the British government.
   d. printed only letters from readers.

6. The most important aspect of colonial life was
   a. family.
   b. school.
   c. farming.
   d. work.

7. One effect of the Great Awakening was that
   a. people relied more on one another.
   b. people became more dependent on the spiritual teachings of preachers.
   c. many small churches closed.
   d. it helped people to see all religions as equally important.

8. Schools were harder to establish in the South because
   a. fewer towns existed in the South.
   b. the settlers in the South were more spread out.
   c. farm work demanded much more of a boy's time than school did.
   d. all of the above

Critical Thinking

Evaluate
On a separate sheet of paper, list the buildings you might find in a typical colonial town. Include at least four places and explain why you chose them.

Section III. Slavery in the Colonies

Write *true* or *false* on the line below each sentence. If the sentence is false, rewrite it to make it true. Use a separate sheet of paper if you need more space.

1. Most enslaved people lived on plantations in the northern colonies.

_____

2. Enslaved people did not own weapons and were very closely watched by their overseers.

_____

3. According to the slave codes, enslaved Africans were encouraged to gather in public.

_____

4. Slave codes were part of the laws in all the British colonies.

_____

5. Under the slave codes, children of enslaved Africans were not themselves considered enslaved.

_____

6. As a result of the Stono Rebellion, enslaved people in South Carolina were given more freedom.

_____

7. Between 1700 and 1750, the number of enslaved Africans living in the colonies decreased.

_____

Critical Thinking

Evaluate
Think about the laws that were enforced under the colonial slave codes. Why do you think that enslaved people were not allowed to learn to read and write? Explain your answer on a separate sheet of paper.

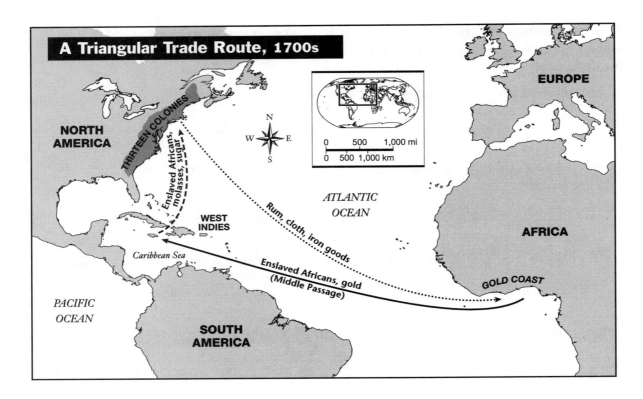

A Triangular Trade Route, 1700s

Use the map to answer the following questions.

1. What did ships transport from the colonies to Africa?

_____

2. What direction did the ships travel to go from the West Indies to the 13 colonies?

_____

3. What ocean did ships cross on the journey from the 13 colonies to Africa?

_____

4. What did ships transport from the West Indies to the 13 colonies?

_____

Choose the answer that best completes each of the following sentences. Circle the letter of the correct answer.

1. Colonial governors were responsible for
   a. making sure the colonists obeyed English laws.
   b. making sure the colonists obeyed laws of the colony.
   c. choosing the members of the council.
   d. all of the above

2. Each colonial government was headed by a
   a. proprietor.
   b. governor.
   c. jury.
   d. customs official.

3. Each colonial government included a(n)
   a. governor.
   b. assembly.
   c. council.
   d. all of the above

4. The replacement of King James II by William of Orange and Mary was called
   a. the Glorious Revolution.
   b. the Magna Carta.
   c. the English Bill of Rights.
   d. the Parliament.

5. The first document to limit the power of English monarchs was
   a. the Glorious Revolution.
   b. the Magna Carta.
   c. the English Bill of Rights.
   d. the Parliament.

6. The purpose of the English Bill of Rights was to
   a. make Parliament more powerful than the monarch.
   b. limit the powers of governors.
   c. give all colonists the right to vote.
   d. all of the above

7. The philosopher John Locke believed
   a. all people are free and independent.
   b. all people have the right to own property.
   c. governments must protect people's rights.
   d. all of the above

8. At the time the Magna Carta was written, the government of England was headed by a
   a. monarch.
   b. proprietor.
   c. parliament.
   d. governor.

Critical Thinking

Evaluate
As a landowner in colonial America, you have the right to vote. How would you argue against a campaign to give people who do not own land the right to vote? Write your answer on a separate sheet of paper.

Section II. Conflict With the French

Complete each sentence with a term from the box.

King George's War	New France	forts	balance of power
King William's War	New England	Catholics	

1. French officials built a series of _____ to serve as military headquarters, missions, and trading posts.

2. Geographically, _____ was much larger than all of the English colonies combined.

3. In Queen Anne's War, colonists in _____ fought French troops and their Native American allies.

4. After Spain, France, and England fought three wars over colonial territory, the _____ in North America did not change very much.

5. King Louis XIV encouraged French _____ to move to New France beginning in 1661.

6. In _____, France joined Spain in fighting the British over colonial trade.

7. When _____ ended in 1697, France and England agreed to return all captured territory.

Critical Thinking

Recognize Relationships
Why were the English colonists unfriendly toward the French? Write your answer on a separate sheet of paper.

Complete the chart below. Give two details for each main idea.
The first one is done for you.

Main Idea	Details
A. Both the British and the French claim the Ohio River Valley.	**1.** *King George II grants 200,000 acres of the region to Virginia business owners.* **2.**
B. British troops and American colonists, with help from the Iroquois, win the war.	**3.** **4.**
C. Great Britain becomes the supreme power in North America.	**5.** **6.**

Critical Thinking

Evaluate
Why was it important for the colonies to unite against the French during the French and Indian War? Write your answer on a separate sheet of paper.

Use the map to answer the following questions.

1. Which French forts were located in or on the border of disputed territory?

_____

2. Which British forts were located in or on the border of disputed territory?

_____

3. Which French fort was located on the eastern shore of Lake Erie?

_____

4. Which nation claimed the territory that included the city of Halifax?

_____

Section I. Resistance to British Taxes

A. Match each item with its description. Write the correct letter on the line.

_____ **1.** meeting in New York to take action against the Stamp Act

_____ **2.** group that protested against the Stamp Act

_____ **3.** a protest in which people refuse to buy certain goods

_____ **4.** an act that required colonists to feed and house British soldiers

_____ **5.** law that placed a tax on non-British imports of sugar, cloth, and coffee

_____ **6.** an official government announcement that prevented colonists from settling west of the Appalachian Mountains

_____ **7.** law that placed a tax on all printed material

_____ **8.** law that gave Parliament the power to tax the colonists for any reason

a. Sugar Act

b. boycott

c. Stamp Act

d. Sons of Liberty

e. Declaratory Act

f. Stamp Act Congress

g. Quartering Act

h. Proclamation of 1763

B. Number the events below in the order in which they occurred.

_____ **9.** The Declaratory Act is passed by British lawmakers.

_____ **10.** British and colonial forces join together to defend settlements against the Native Americans led by Pontiac.

_____ **11.** The French and Indian War ends.

_____ **12.** The Molasses Act is passed by Parliament.

Critical Thinking

Evaluate
Do you think the colonists had a right to settle in lands west of the Appalachian Mountains? Write your answer on a separate sheet of paper.

Section II. Growing Tensions

Complete each sentence with a term from the box.

Townshend Acts	resolutions	Boston Tea Party
Boston Massacre	Intolerable Acts	Tea Act
Committee of Correspondence	Quebec Act	

1. The colonial legislature in Virginia issued _____ stating that

only it had the right to tax its citizens.

2. The _____ took place when a crowd of colonists threw rocks

and snowballs at British customs officers and soldiers.

3. After the Stamp Act was repealed, Parliament passed the _____

to collect taxes to pay off Great Britain's war debt.

4. The _____ was a protest by the Sons of Liberty.

5. The Coercive Acts, which closed the port of Boston as punishment for the Boston

Tea Party, were called the _____ by the colonists.

6. Parliament replaced the Townshend Acts with the _____.

7. Samuel Adams started the _____ to let colonists know about

British actions in Boston.

8. The British took western lands north of the Ohio River away from the colonists by

passing the _____.

Critical Thinking

Evaluate

You are a colonist who does not agree with the new
taxes. Why do you disagree with the Townshend Acts?
Write your answer on a separate sheet of paper.

7 Section III. A Declaration of Independence

Write *true* or *false* on the line below each sentence. If the sentence is false, rewrite it to make it true. Use a separate sheet of paper if you need more space.

1. The first battles in the war with Great Britain took place at Lexington and Concord.

   _____

2. The Olive Branch Petition was the colonists' second attempt to get King George to stop the fighting and try to reach an agreement with them.

   _____

3. Colonial leaders met in Philadelphia for the First Continental Congress.

   _____

4. When King George received the first petition from the First Continental Congress, he told Parliament to force the colonies to obey the British laws.

   _____

5. The delegates to the First Continental Congress decided to use Benjamin Franklin's idea for a plan to bring the colonies together.

   _____

6. The purpose of the Declaration of Independence was to declare war on Great Britain.

   _____

7. Thomas Paine argued that the colonists should not only protect their rights as British subjects but also fight for the cause of liberty.

   _____

Critical Thinking

Evaluate
Write a news article about the First Continental Congress. Include *who? what? when? where?* and *why?* Write your article on a separate sheet of paper.

Use the map to answer the following questions.

1. Which nation controlled the island of Cuba?

_____

2. Which nation controlled the lands west of the Mississippi River?

_____

3. Which nation controlled the five Great Lakes?

_____

4. Which body or bodies of water bordered the land controlled by the British colonies?

_____

Declaration of Independence Handbook

A. Study the Declaration of Independence on pages 157–161 of your textbook. Answer the questions on the lines below. Use a separate sheet of paper if you need more space.

1. The colonists had good reasons for declaring independence. Take a stand to agree or disagree with this statement.

   _____

   _____

2. The makers of the Declaration proposed a new form of government in the Preamble. Describe this new government.

   _____

   _____

3. The colonists used the document to explain why the colonies should be independent. Choose one section. Identify and explain three of the colonists' complaints.

   _____

   _____

4. Do you think people under the age of 18 should have the right to vote? Use ideas that are in the Declaration to make an argument.

   _____

   _____

B. Choose one of the following essay topics. Write your answer in a paragraph on a separate sheet of paper.

5. One of the most famous phrases in the Declaration of Independence states that "all men are created equal." Do you think this phrase applied to all people living in the colonies? Explain.

6. Write a journal entry describing what your life might be like if the Declaration of Independence had never been written. What rights would you or would you not have? Would your daily life change? Explain.

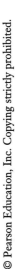

Complete the chart below. Fill in information about the American and British sides during the Revolutionary War. Some of the chart is filled in for you.

Side	Advantages	Sites of Victories
Americans	1. They were familiar with the land. 2.	5. 6.
British	3. 4.	7. 8.

Critical Thinking

Draw Conclusions
Patriots were very passionate about fighting for their freedom. Why do you think some colonists did not want independence from Great Britain? Write your answer on a separate sheet of paper.

Section II. The War Expands

Complete the cause/effect chart below with sentences from the box.

> British troops retreat to Saratoga to wait for reinforcements.
>
> George Washington retreats to Valley Forge.
>
> American troops run out of supplies and surrender at Charleston.
>
> Patriots suffer from cold and hunger at Valley Forge.
>
> The Patriot victory at Saratoga shows they can win the war.
>
> The British army lost many troops in a battle in the Carolinas.

Cause	Effect
British troops win the battle at Brandywine Creek.	1.
2.	George Washington took supplies and food from nearby farms.
The militia travels across New England to fight General Burgoyne.	3.
4.	France signed treaties to aid Patriots at war.
The British navy controls the waters around South Carolina.	5.
6.	General Cornwallis decides to head north to Virginia.

Critical Thinking

Make Inferences
What might have happened if General Howe and his troops had joined General Burgoyne as planned? Explain your answer on a separate sheet of paper.

A. Match each item with its description. Write the correct letter on the line.

_____ **1.** the British general who was defeated in the final battle of the Revolutionary War

a. Treaty of Paris

_____ **2.** agreement that recognized the independence of the United States of America

b. United States of America

_____ **3.** the first nation to be founded on the ideal and goal of equal rights

c. republic

_____ **4.** a nation that aided the Americans in the Revolutionary War

d. Benedict Arnold

_____ **5.** a nation in which the citizens hold supreme power

e. inflation

_____ **6.** the general who returned to Virginia after the war to become a civilian

f. Charles Cornwallis

_____ **7.** a sharp increase in the price of goods and services

g. George Washington

_____ **8.** the American general who turned over West Point to the British

h. France

B. Number the events below in the order in which they occurred.

_____ **9.** George Washington gathers his officers together in New York for a farewell dinner.

_____ **10.** Benedict Arnold switches sides and joins the British forces.

_____ **11.** Benedict Arnold is placed in command of West Point.

_____ **12.** The Treaty of Paris is signed.

Critical Thinking

Synthesize Information
You are a newspaper reporter in New York during George Washington's farewell dinner. What are three questions you would ask General Washington? Write your questions on a separate sheet of paper.

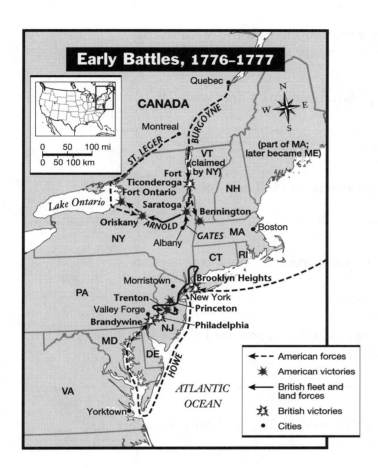

Use the map to answer the following questions.

1. Where did the American troops go when they left Montreal, Canada?

_____

_____

2. Which of the battles shown on the map were won by the Americans?

_____

_____

3. Which of the battles shown on the map were won by the British?

_____

_____

4. About how many miles was the route from Quebec to Fort Ticonderoga?

_____

Section I. The First Government

**Write *true* or *false* on the line below each sentence. If the sentence is
false, rewrite it to make it true. Use a separate sheet of paper if you
need more space.**

1. Thomas Jefferson believed that the government's main duty was to tell
   people what to think.

   _____

2. Most Americans wanted to create a monarchy in the United States.

   _____

3. The Articles of Confederation allowed for a president and a court system.

   _____

4. Maryland refused to ratify the Articles of Confederation until all the states
   gave up their claims to western land.

   _____

5. Under the Articles of Confederation, Congress had the authority to collect
   money through taxes.

   _____

6. Many Americans were afraid to establish a strong federal government and
   wanted each state to keep its full sovereignty.

   _____

7. Americans decided to create a republic, which allowed citizens to elect their leaders.

   _____

Critical Thinking

Synthesize Information
What was the purpose of the Articles of Confederation?
On a separate sheet of paper, list two of its strengths
and two of its weaknesses.

Complete the chart below by writing two facts about each ordinance. The first one has been done for you.

Ordinance	Facts
Ordinance of 1784	**1.** *The United States would add to the number of independent states in the country.* **2.**
Ordinance of 1785	**3.** **4.**
Northwest Ordinance of 1785	**5.** **6.**

Critical Thinking

Synthesize Information

You are a farmer living in Massachusetts. Daniel Shays has asked you to join his rebellion. Decide if you will or will not join him. Then, write a letter to Shays explaining your choice. Write your letter on a separate sheet of paper.

A. Choose the answer that best completes each of the following sentences. Circle the letter of the correct answer.

1. Delegates at the Constitutional Convention wrote a

   a. treaty to end the rebellion in Massachusetts.

   b. charter to reduce the size of the federal government.

   c. law establishing new state lines.

   d. constitution that created a stronger federal government.

2. The New Jersey Plan called for

   a. rewards for small states.

   b. penalties for large states.

   c. equal representation for all states.

   d. representation based on population.

3. Federalists

   a. supported a strong federal government.

   b. refused to ratify the Constitution.

   c. wanted more power for the states.

   d. argued that each state should have equal representation in Congress.

4. Only Congress can

   a. appoint federal officials.

   b. veto laws.

   c. decide if a law is constitutional.

   d. declare war.

5. The purpose of checks and balances is to

   a. maintain a balanced federal budget for the country.

   b. prevent one branch of government from becoming too powerful.

   c. allow the President to take control of the judicial branch.

   d. permit Congress to rule in the President's absence.

6. The first ten amendments to the Constitution are called the

   a. Federalist Documents.

   b. Constitutional Freedoms.

   c. Bill of Rights.

   d. Constitutional Compromise.

B. Number the events below in the order in which they occurred.

_____ 7. New Hampshire becomes the ninth state to ratify the Constitution.

_____ 8. Ten amendments are added to the Constitution.

_____ 9. Delegates sign the U.S. Constitution.

Critical Thinking

Draw Conclusions
Did the Founding Fathers of the U.S. Constitution guarantee freedom for all people? Explain your answer on a separate sheet of paper.

The Northwest Territory, 1787

CANADA
(Great Britain)

Lake Superior

Minnesota
(1858)

Mississippi R.

Wisconsin
(1848)

Lake Michigan

Lake Huron

Lake Ontario

LOUISIANA
(Spain)

N
W   E
S

Michigan
(1837)

Lake Erie

NY

PA

(1848) Date of admission
to the United States

Northwest Territory

Present-day state
boundaries

0   100   200 mi
0   100   200 km

Illinois
(1818)

Indiana
(1816)

Ohio
(1803)

VA

Ohio R.

KY

Use the map to answer the following questions.

1. List the states in the Northwest Territory by the year they were admitted to the United States. Begin with the first state admitted.

_____

_____

2. Which river flows along the western border of the Northwest Territory?

_____

3. Which Spanish territory is located west of the Northwest Territory?

_____

4. Which country is located north of the Great Lakes?

_____

⭐ 9 Constitution Handbook

A. **Study the U.S. Constitution on pages 214–239 of your textbook. Answer the questions on the lines below. Use a separate sheet of paper if you need more space.**

1. What is the purpose of the Preamble to the Constitution?

_____

_____

_____

_____

2. What is the role of each branch of government under the Constitution?

_____

_____

_____

_____

3. Study the amendments to the Constitution. Which do you think are most important? Why?

_____

_____

_____

_____

B. **Choose one of the following essay topics. Write your answer in a paragraph on a separate sheet of paper.**

4. The Constitution specifies that only natural-born citizens may serve as President. Do you think this is a fair requirement? Write a newspaper editorial explaining your answer. Include examples or reasons to support your opinion.

5. Do you think the Thirteenth, Fifteenth, and Nineteenth Amendments reflect changes in society's beliefs? Explain.

Answer each question on the lines below.

1. Which departments made up the nation's first Cabinet?

_____

2. Where was the country's capital moved to?

_____

3. What specific powers did the Constitution give to Congress?

_____

4. Who was the first justice of the Supreme Court?

_____

5. Why did Alexander Hamilton want the federal government to pay off its debt?

_____

6. Who was the first Secretary of War?

_____

7. Why did southern states oppose helping the federal government repay its debts?

_____

8. Who was the first President of the United States?

_____

Critical Thinking

Analyze Primary Sources
What do you see as a possible benefit and drawback of the Constitution's "elastic clause"? Explain your answer on a separate sheet of paper.

Complete each sentence with a term from the box.

Federalist Party	loose interpretation	Treaty of Greenville
Democratic-Republican Party	whiskey	state governments
French Revolution	Jay's Treaty	

1. Thomas Jefferson wanted to place as much power as possible in the hands of

_____.

2. Alexander Hamilton believed in a _____ of the Constitution.

3. People who supported the _____ believed in a strong

national government and the importance of industry.

4. In 1794, some farmers in western Pennsylvania expressed outrage over a tax on

_____.

5. The _____ wanted a limited national government and

stronger state governments.

6. Alexander Hamilton and Thomas Jefferson disagreed over how the United States

should react to the _____.

7. _____ attempted to ease tensions between Great Britain

and the United States.

8. Native Americans were forced to sign the _____ in 1795.

Critical Thinking

Evaluate
You are asked to join either the Federalists or the Democratic-Republicans. Write a paragraph on a separate sheet of paper explaining your decision.

Complete the cause/effect chain below. Write the causes and effects for each event.

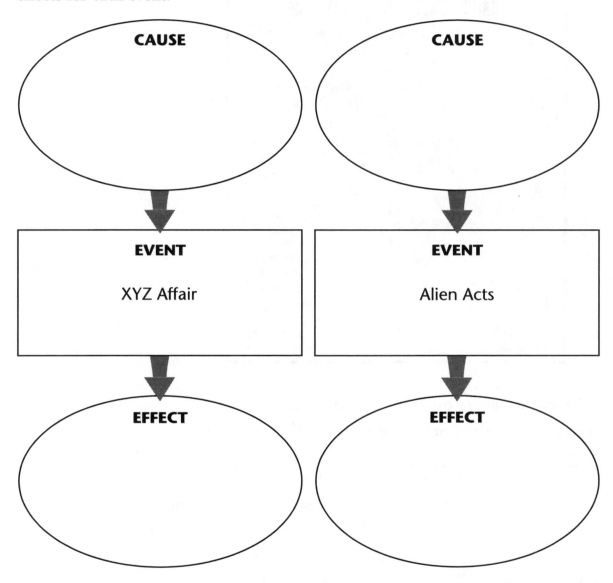

CAUSE

CAUSE

EVENT

XYZ Affair

EVENT

Alien Acts

EFFECT

EFFECT

Critical Thinking

Evaluate

Do you agree with the beliefs of supporters of states' rights? Explain your answer on a separate sheet of paper.

The United States, 1796

Use the map to answer the following questions.

1. In what year did Vermont become part of the United States?

_____

2. Which bodies of water form a border between New York and Canada?

_____

3. In what year did the Battle of Fallen Timbers take place?

_____

4. Which area on the map belonged to Great Britain?

_____

11 Section I. Jefferson as President

Answer each question on the lines below.

1. Why did the Federalists invite Aaron Burr to run for governor of New York?

_____

2. Why did Aaron Burr challenge Alexander Hamilton to a duel?

_____

3. What was the main reason why John Adams lost his bid for re-election in 1800?

_____

4. Why did John Adams consider Thomas Jefferson a radical?

_____

5. In the presidential election of 1800, how was the tie in the electoral college broken?

_____

6. What was the difference in the way the electoral college operated before and after the Twelfth Amendment to the Constitution was passed?

_____

7. What was Thomas Jefferson's view of government?

_____

8. What important change resulted from the *Marbury* v. *Madison* case?

_____

Critical Thinking

Recognize Relationships
When Thomas Jefferson was elected President, he appointed Democratic-Republicans to positions that had been held by Federalists. On a separate sheet of paper, explain the effects of this transfer of power.

11 Section II. The Louisiana Purchase

A. Number the events below in the order in which they occurred.

_____ **1.** The United States purchases the Louisiana Territory from France.

_____ **2.** The Lewis and Clark expedition comes to an end in St. Louis.

_____ **3.** Congress passes the Embargo Act of 1807, which requires U.S. ships to stop trading with European countries.

_____ **4.** The United States stops paying tribute to the other Barbary states.

_____ **5.** Meriwether Lewis and William Clark set off to explore the Louisiana Territory.

B. Complete the chart below with information about the Louisiana Purchase. One has been filled in for you.

The Louisiana Purchase	
Who?	
What?	
Where?	
When?	_April 30, 1803_
Why?	

Critical Thinking

Synthesize Information
You are preparing to go with Lewis and Clark on their expedition into the Louisiana Territory. Write a letter to a friend explaining why the expedition has been formed, what you and the other explorers plan to do, and some of the preparations you are making for the journey. Write your letter on a separate sheet of paper.

A. **Match each item with its description. Write the correct letter on the line.**

_____ **1.** group in Congress who wanted to fight against Great Britain

_____ **2.** Shawnee leader who wanted to drive all settlers out of the Northwest Territory

_____ **3.** one of the leaders of the War Hawks

_____ **4.** President during the War of 1812

_____ **5.** the poem written to celebrate the fact that Fort McHenry's flag was still flying

_____ **6.** person who successfully defended New Orleans against a British attack

_____ **7.** treaty that brought an end to the War of 1812

_____ **8.** pride in one's country

a. James Madison

b. Major General Andrew Jackson

c. nationalism

d. Tecumseh

e. War Hawks

f. Treaty of Ghent

g. John C. Calhoun

h. "The Star-Spangled Banner"

B. **Number the events below in the order in which they occurred.**

_____ **9.** The United States passes a law allowing U.S. ships to trade with any country except Great Britain or France.

_____ **10.** The Treaty of Ghent is signed.

_____ **11.** The Americans gain control of Lake Erie.

_____ **12.** The United States begins war with Great Britain.

Critical Thinking

Evaluate
Write a memo that the War Hawks might have sent to President Madison explaining why they wanted to declare war on Great Britain. Write your memo on a separate sheet of paper.

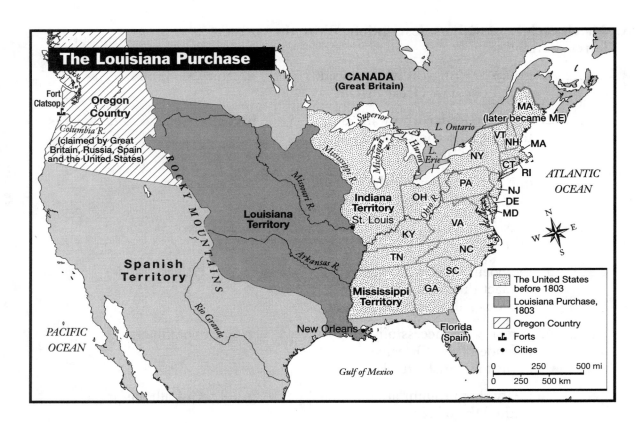

The Louisiana Purchase

Use the map to answer the following questions.

1. Which rivers run through the Louisiana Territory?

_____

2. Which city is located where the Mississippi River flows into the Gulf of Mexico?

_____

3. Which fort is located in the Oregon Country?

_____

4. Which state in the United States reached farthest west before 1803?

_____

12 Section I. The Rise of Nationalism

A. Complete the chart below. Write three details about the American System.

The American System
1.
2.
3.

B. Answer the questions on the lines below.

4. Why was the presidency of James Monroe known as the "Era of Good Feelings"?

_____

5. Which states joined the Union between 1812 and 1819?

_____

6. How did the Supreme Court's decision in *Gibbons* v. *Ogden* help to strengthen the federal government?

_____

Critical Thinking

Make Inferences
How do you think European leaders of the 1820s reacted to the Monroe Doctrine? Write your answer on a separate sheet of paper.

Complete the chart below. Write two details for each main idea.
The first one is done for you.

Main Idea	Details
A. Andrew Jackson was viewed as a man of the people.	**1.** *Jackson grew up in the backwoods of South Carolina and educated himself.* **2.**
B. The election of Andrew Jackson brought great changes to American politics.	**3.** **4.**
C. Andrew Jackson battled the Bank of the United States.	**5.** **6.**

Critical Thinking

Synthesize Information
You are a journalist writing an article about Andrew Jackson. Summarize what you feel were the most important things that he did as President. Write your article on a separate sheet of paper.

Write *true* or *false* on the line below each sentence. If the sentence is false, rewrite it to make it true. Use a separate sheet of paper if you need more space.

1. Most English settlers tried to live in peace with Native Americans.

   _____

2. In the 1820s and 1830s, the U.S. government began a policy of sharing land with Native Americans in the East.

   _____

3. The Great Plains is the mountainous eastern region of the United States.

   _____

4. Andrew Jackson was against relocating Native Americans to the West.

   _____

5. The Indian Removal Act ordered Native Americans to give up their lands east of the Mississippi River in exchange for land west of the river.

   _____

6. The Supreme Court ruled that the Cherokees had to give up control of their land in Georgia.

   _____

7. The 800-mile march of the Seminole people to Indian Territory became known as the Trail of Tears.

   _____

Critical Thinking

Evaluate
Write a speech to President Jackson opposing the Indian Removal Act. Write your speech on a separate sheet of paper.

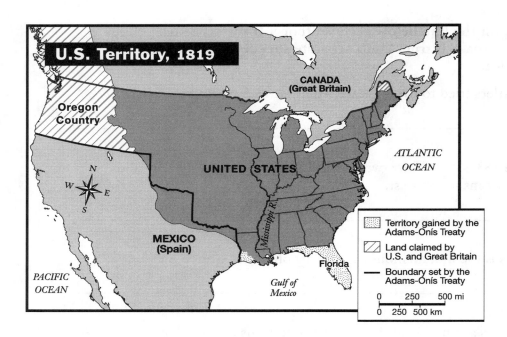

Use the map to answer the following questions.

1. Which countries claimed the Oregon Country?

_____

2. Which bodies of water bordered territory gained by the Adams-Onís Treaty?

_____

3. Between which two countries did the Adams-Onís Treaty establish a boundary?

_____

4. Which country controlled Mexico?

_____

13 Section I. The Industrial Revolution

Answer each question on the lines below.

1. What was the first use for Eli Whitney's concept of interchangeable parts?

_____

2. What were two inventions that made farming easier?

_____

3. Who made up Francis Lowell's new labor system?

_____

4. Before the Industrial Revolution, how were most goods made?

_____

5. How did the War of 1812 and the Tariff of 1816 lead to an increase in the number of American factories?

_____

6. How did Great Britain try to keep its industrialization efforts a secret?

_____

7. Why did industrialization rely on improved transportation?

_____

8. How did the invention of the telegraph improve communications?

_____

Critical Thinking

Recognize Relationships
Industrial growth primarily took place in the northern states. How did the southern states contribute to this growth? Write your answer on a separate sheet of paper.

Complete each sentence with a term from the box.

planter	Cotton Kingdom	seeds	cotton gins
plantation system	cash crop	tariffs	textile

1. Removing the _____ from a few pounds of short-staple

cotton often took a worker a whole day.

2. By the 1830s, cotton was the major _____ of numerous

southern states.

3. A _____ was a person who owned and operated a plantation.

4. Without slavery, the _____ would have collapsed.

5. The _____ industry in New England benefited from the

South's increased cotton production.

6. The area as far west as Texas and north into Virginia was known as the

_____.

7. Southerners protested the nation's high _____, which

made it expensive to buy goods from other countries.

8. Owners of large plantations often built _____ powered by

horses or mules, rather than by a hand crank.

Critical Thinking

Evaluate
Name at least three ways that the North differed from
the South by the mid-1800s. Write your answer on a
separate sheet of paper.

13 Section III. The Slave System

Write *true* or *false* on the line below each sentence. If the sentence is false, rewrite it to make it true. Use a separate sheet of paper if you need more space.

1. Enslaved people lived in all of the original British colonies, but most lived in the North.

   _____

2. Slave codes made sure that enslaved people had all the basic freedoms that other U.S. citizens enjoyed.

   _____

3. Most enslaved African Americans endured long hours of work in the fields.

   _____

4. Because laws did not recognize slave marriages, few enslaved African American men and women developed strong family ties.

   _____

5. Enslaved African Americans saw little need for religion in their lives.

   _____

6. Some conductors on the Underground Railroad were Northerners opposed to slavery.

   _____

7. After Turner's Rebellion, the South passed stricter slave codes and took harsher measures to prevent more uprisings.

   _____

Critical Thinking

Recognize Relationships
How did the invention of the cotton gin and the development of plantations change ideas about slavery in the South? Write your answer on a separate sheet of paper.

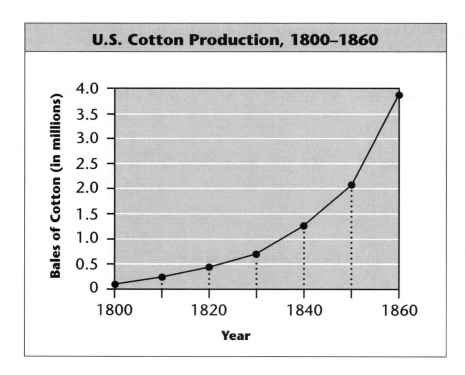

U.S. Cotton Production, 1800–1860

Use the graph to answer the following questions.

1. What does the graph show?

_____

2. Between which twenty-year period did cotton production increase the most?

_____

3. By which year had cotton production surpassed one million bales?

_____

4. About how many bales of cotton were produced in 1850?

_____

5. What trend do you see reflected in the graph?

_____

Complete each sentence with a term from the box.

enslaved people	public education	government	overcrowded
American Party	immigrants	diversity	nativism

1. Because there was not enough housing for all the newcomers, cities became

_____.

2. _____ from foreign countries increased the population

of the United States in the 1800s.

3. Horace Mann felt that taxes should support a _____ system.

4. In many states, it was against the law to teach _____ how to

read and write.

5. Because each group of immigrants brought some part of its culture with them, the

_____ of the United States began to grow.

6. The _____ tried to limit immigration.

7. Increased immigration produced a negative reaction among some Americans known as

_____.

8. The U.S. _____ encouraged immigration because these new

Americans could fill jobs created by the growing number of factories and businesses.

Critical Thinking

Synthesize Information
Name the positive and negative effects that
increased immigration had on the United States.
Write your answer on a separate sheet of paper.

Choose the answer that best completes each of the following sentences. Circle the letter of the correct answer.

1. Some Americans became writers in the 1830s because
   a. they were freed from Great Britain.
   b. the Constitution was written.
   c. the audience of readers grew.
   d. immigrants arrived on the eastern coast.

2. The European writer who used the Americas as a setting for a perfect society was
   a. Alexis de Tocqueville.
   b. Sir Thomas More.
   c. Washington Irving.
   d. John J. Audubon.

3. In his essay "Self-Reliance," Ralph Waldo Emerson showed his belief in
   a. transcendentalism.
   b. democracy.
   c. equality.
   d. slavery.

4. All of the following people wrote American literature except
   a. Herman Melville.
   b. Walt Whitman.
   c. James Fenimore Cooper.
   d. Stephen C. Foster.

5. Harriet Beecher Stowe's *Uncle Tom's Cabin* focused on the cruelty of
   a. prisons.
   b. slavery.
   c. urban life.
   d. nativism.

6. The Hudson River school was a new movement in American
   a. painting.
   b. writing.
   c. music.
   d. science.

7. John J. Audubon advanced science with his beautiful drawings of
   a. the sky.
   b. trees.
   c. birds.
   d. animals.

8. Washington Irving wrote one of the first biographies of
   a. George Washington.
   b. Benjamin Franklin.
   c. Thomas Jefferson.
   d. John Adams.

Critical Thinking

Synthesize Information
Write an editorial about literature in the United States. What beliefs and attitudes does American writing show? Write your editorial on a separate sheet of paper.

Section III. Reforming Society

Complete the chart below. Write facts about each of the reforms listed.
The first one is done for you.

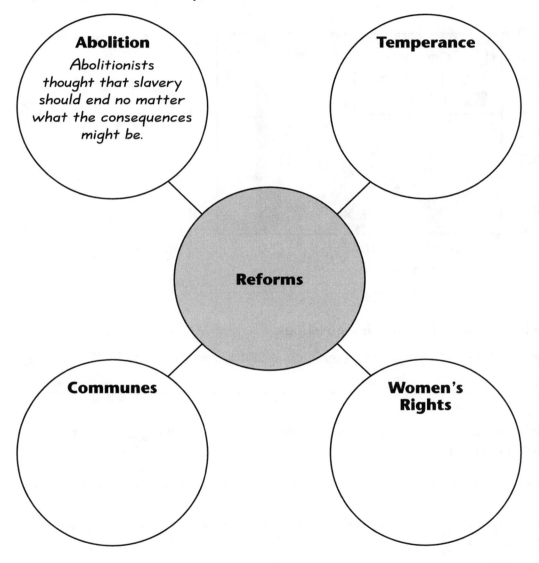

Abolition
Abolitionists thought that slavery should end no matter what the consequences might be.

Temperance

Reforms

Communes

Women's Rights

Critical Thinking

Evaluate
Compare and contrast the women's rights and abolition movements. What was similar and different about the goals of the two movements and how each movement fought for them? Write your answer on a separate sheet of paper.

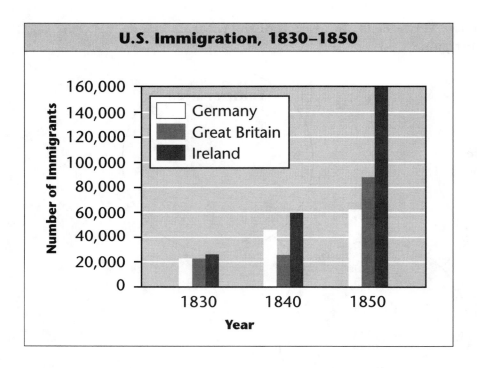

U.S. Immigration, 1830–1850

Use the graph to answer the following questions.

1. About how many people immigrated to the United States from Germany in 1840?

_____

2. In which year was the number of immigrants from Germany much higher than the number from Great Britain?

_____

3. About how many immigrants came to the United States in 1830 from Germany and Great Britain combined?

_____

4. About how many immigrants came to the United States in 1850 from Ireland and Great Britain combined?

_____

Section I. Texas Wins Independence

Answer each question on the lines below.

1. What brought settlers to Texas?

_____

2. Why did Texas settlers and Mexican authorities clash?

_____

3. How did Mexican authorities try to take greater control over Texas?

_____

4. Which side won the Battle of the Alamo?

_____

5. Why did Texas want to join the United States?

_____

6. Why did Congress initially reject the annexation of Texas?

_____

7. Why did some Americans want Texas to join the United States?

_____

8. How did James Knox Polk feel about the annexation of Texas?

_____

Critical Thinking

Recognize Relationships
How was the action taken by the American settlers in Texas like the action taken by the American colonists in the Revolutionary War? Explain your answer on a separate sheet of paper.

Section II. War With Mexico and the Movement West

A. Match each item with its description. Write the correct letter on the line.

_____ **1.** the founder of the Mormon religion

_____ **2.** a popular western path followed by American settlers

_____ **3.** area of land claimed by the United States and Great Britain

_____ **4.** a treaty made between the U.S. government and Native American groups

_____ **5.** the dividing line that split the Oregon Territory

a. Oregon Trail

b. forty-ninth parallel

c. Joseph Smith

d. Treaty of Fort Laramie

e. Oregon Territory

B. Complete the chart below. Write the causes of the War with Mexico.

Causes of the War With Mexico
6.
7.
8.
9.

Critical Thinking

Evaluate

You are a settler following the Oregon Trail. Write a journal entry describing your trip from Independence, Missouri, to Fort Vancouver. Write your journal entry on a separate sheet of paper.

15 Section III. Settlement in California

Complete each sentence with a term from the box.

John Sutter	church	companies	farming
slavery	presidio	towns	Father Junipero Serra

1. The first _____ built by the Spaniards was located in the present-day city of San Diego.

2. Many Spanish missionaries tried to convince Native Americans to abandon hunting and gathering for _____.

3. As more settlers arrived in California, the development of _____ led to the abandonment of many missions.

4. The owner of the sawmill in California where gold was discovered was _____.

5. Nearly half the missions in northern California were founded by _____.

6. Large _____ made the most money from gold mining.

7. The constitution that was adopted by California in 1849 banned _____.

8. Life in most missions centered around their _____.

Critical Thinking

Draw Conclusions
You are living on the East Coast when the gold rush begins. Would you join the rush to California? Explain your answer on a separate sheet of paper.

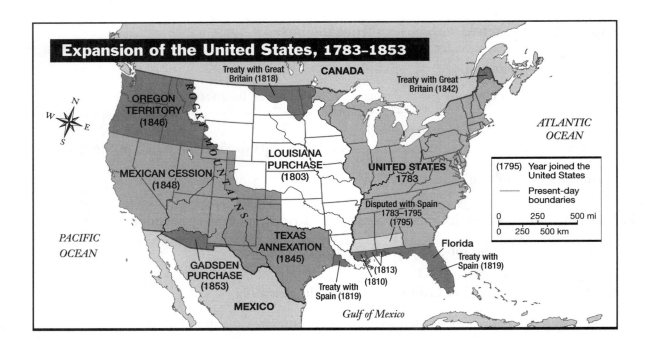

Expansion of the United States, 1783–1853

Use the map to answer the following questions.

1. When was Texas annexed?

_____

2. What area was added to the United States in 1803?

_____

3. Which country formed the southern border of the Gadsden Purchase?

_____

4. Which country formed the northern boundary of the Oregon Territory?

_____

5. In what year did the Oregon Territory become part of the United States?

_____

Section I. The Question of Slavery in the West

A. Complete the chart below with information about the Missouri Compromise and the Compromise of 1850. Some of the chart is filled in for you.

Two Important Compromises	
The Missouri Compromise	**The Compromise of 1850**
1. *Missouri would join the Union as a slaveholding state.*	4.
2.	5. *The slave trade would end in Washington, D.C.*
3.	6.

B. Answer each question on the lines below.

7. Which kind of government did the North want?

_____

8. Which kind of government did the South want?

_____

Critical Thinking

Evaluate
The lawmakers John C. Calhoun, Henry Clay, and David Wilmot each had a different approach to handling the slavery issue. Describe each of their approaches.
Write your answer on a separate sheet of paper.

Write *true* or *false* on the line below each sentence. If the sentence is false, rewrite it to make it true. Use a separate sheet of paper if you need more space.

1. Abolitionists in the North helped enslaved people escape to freedom on the Underground Railroad.

   _____

2. The Missouri Compromise required Northerners to help capture escaped slaves and return them to slaveholders in the South.

   _____

3. Harriet Beecher Stowe's novel *Uncle Tom's Cabin* helped people throughout the world understand that slavery was a human problem.

   _____

4. Border ruffians were extremists who helped elect a proslavery government in Kansas.

   _____

5. Senator Stephen Douglas did not support the Kansas-Nebraska Act.

   _____

6. In 1856, the violence in Kansas gave the territory the nickname Bleeding Kansas.

   _____

7. In the Dred Scott case, the Supreme Court ruled that Scott could not file a lawsuit because African Americans were not citizens.

   _____

Critical Thinking

Evaluate
Under the Fugitive Slave Law, Northerners who assisted runaway slaves faced a six-month jail term and a $1,000 fine. Why do you think some Northerners broke this law? Write your answer on a separate sheet of paper.

Section III. Challenges to Slavery

Complete each sentence with a term from the box.

slavery	Charles Sumner	popular sovereignty	secede
Free-Soil	Alabama Platform	Harpers Ferry	emancipate

1. Before the 1850s, political parties such as the _____

   Party and the Whigs formed to oppose the spread of slavery.

2. The Republican Party included many abolitionists who wanted to

   _____ the enslaved people.

3. After Senator _____ ridiculed Senator Andrew Butler

   in a speech to the Senate, he was attacked by a relative of Butler's.

4. The Republican Party opposed Stephen Douglas because he supported

   _____.

5. John Brown led a group of followers on a raid of the federal arsenal in

   _____.

6. The Democratic Party was divided over the issue of _____.

7. William L. Yancey's proposal asking the Democrats to support slavery in the

   territories was known as the _____.

8. Southerners threatened to _____ if the Republicans won

   the election of 1860.

Critical Thinking

Synthesize Information
Slavery was the main political issue in the Lincoln-Douglas debates. What are some important topics of debate today? Write your answer on a separate sheet of paper.

Section IV. Breaking Away From the Union

A. **Number the following groups of events in the order in which they occurred. The first one is done for you.**

1. _____ **a.** South Carolina is the first state to secede from the Union.

   _____ **b.** Six more states join South Carolina and secede.

   _____ **c.** The states that seceded create the Confederate States of America.

   __1__ **d.** Abraham Lincoln wins the election of 1860.

2. _____ **a.** Confederate forces open fire on Fort Sumter, and the Union commander surrenders.

   __1__ **b.** Jefferson Davis is elected as provisional president of the Confederacy.

   _____ **c.** Confederate officials demand that federal property within their states be handed over to the Confederate government.

   _____ **d.** The Committee of 33 and the Committee of 13 work to find a compromise to restore the Union.

B. **Match each item with its description. Write the correct letter on the line.**

_____ **3.** site where the Civil War began   **a.** line item veto

_____ **4.** part of this plan included a promise of payment for runaway slaves if the Fugitive Slave Law was not enforced properly   **b.** Montgomery, Alabama

_____ **5.** a veto of a portion but not all of a proposed law   **c.** Fort Sumter

_____ **6.** original site of the Confederate government   **d.** Crittenden Compromise

Critical Thinking

Evaluate

Why do you think President Lincoln and Congress worked so hard to keep the Union together? Explain your answer on a separate sheet of paper.

The Election of 1860

Candidate	Total Electoral	Total Popular
Lincoln (Rep.)	180	1,866,452
Breckinridge (Dem.)	72	847,953
Bell (Constit. Union)	39	590,631
Douglas (Dem.)	12	1,375,157

Numbers with states represent electoral votes.

Use the map to answer the following questions.

1. Who won the most electoral votes in the North?

_____

2. Who won the most electoral votes in the South?

_____

3. Which state had the most electoral votes?

_____

4. Which three states were won by Bell?

_____

Choose the answer that best completes each of the following sentences. Circle the letter of the correct answer.

1. The goal of the Anaconda Plan was to
   a. attack relentlessly and win quickly.
   b. cut off supplies and divide the South into two parts.
   c. wage total war on the Confederacy.
   d. attack in a slow and methodical way.

2. One advantage the Confederacy had over the Union was
   a. a larger population.
   b. a stronger economy.
   c. a better transportation network.
   d. control of the cotton crop.

3. Lincoln incorrectly assumed the Union would easily win the Battle of
   a. Bull Run.
   b. Antietam.
   c. Chancellorsville.
   d. Vicksburg.

4. The Confederate capital was located at
   a. Vicksburg, Mississippi.
   b. Richmond, Virginia.
   c. Washington, D.C.
   d. Manassas, Virginia.

5. One state that was not considered a border state was
   a. Maryland.
   b. Virginia.
   c. Missouri.
   d. Kentucky.

6. Nonslaveholding farmers in Virginia formed their own state called
   a. North Carolina.
   b. Tennessee.
   c. West Virginia.
   d. Maryland.

7. Early in the war, the South won most of the battles
   a. at sea.
   b. north of Virginia.
   c. west of the Appalachian Mountains.
   d. east of the Appalachian Mountains.

8. One reason Northerners fought in the war was to
   a. keep slavery legal.
   b. end slavery.
   c. gain independence.
   d. show their support for states' rights.

Critical Thinking

Synthesize Information
Write an editorial about the Civil War from the point of view of a Union supporter or a Confederate supporter. Explain why the war must be fought and what is at stake. Write your editorial on a separate sheet of paper.

17 Section II. War and American Life

A. Complete each sentence on the lines below.

1. Great Britain considered recognizing the Confederacy as a separate nation from the United States because it needed a source of _____.

2. Both the North and the South got more men to fight the battles of the Civil War by passing _____ laws.

3. Soldiers engaged in _____ in the Civil War, 50 years before the practice became common in World War I.

4. The Union's _____ prevented the Confederacy from shipping cotton to Great Britain.

5. Wooden ships in battles of the Civil War were strengthened by covering them with _____.

6. In the _____, President Lincoln ordered that all enslaved people in areas still controlled by the Confederacy would be free.

7. Some people in Great Britain opposed _____ and did not want to help the Confederacy.

8. When soldiers left for war, _____ often took over work in factories, on plantations, or in other businesses to support their families.

Critical Thinking

Recognize Relationships
Discuss why the Confederacy hoped for Great Britain's support and the reasons why Great Britain did not offer its support. Write your answer on a separate sheet of paper.

Section III. Victory for the North

Complete each sentence with a term from the box.

Pickett's Charge	censorship	Vicksburg	Atlanta
Gettysburg	habeas corpus	Wilderness Campaign	

1. Union commander Ulysses S. Grant took control of _____

   after a six-week siege of the city.

2. General Lee hoped to score a decisive victory and gain supplies for his

   troops by winning the battle at _____.

3. Thousands of Confederate soldiers were killed when they stormed across

   an open field in what became known as _____.

4. When people spoke out against the war, President Lincoln suspended

   _____ and imprisoned them without a trial.

5. The government's decision to close more than 300 newspapers for

   criticizing the war was an act of _____.

6. General Grant and General Lee fought a series of battles in Richmond known

   as the _____.

7. As General Grant and General Lee fought for Petersburg, General Sherman

   took 100,000 troops to attack and burn _____.

Critical Thinking

Evaluate
Do you think General Sherman should have brought total war to the South? Explain your answer on a separate sheet of paper.

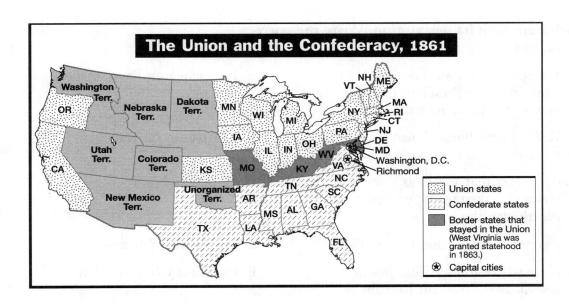

The Union and the Confederacy, 1861

Union states	
Confederate states	
Border states that stayed in the Union (West Virginia was granted statehood in 1863.)	
⊛ Capital cities	

Use the map to answer the following questions.

1. Which were the five border states?

_____

2. Which two Union states were separated from the rest of the Union by territories?

_____

3. Which city was the capital of the Confederacy?

_____

4. Which city was the capital of the Union?

_____

5. What were the six named territories?

_____

Match each item with its description. Write the correct letter on the line.

_____ 1. the person who was nominated as Lincoln's Vice President in 1864 as a way to promote national unity

a. Emancipation Proclamation

_____ 2. Radical Republicans' plan for reuniting the North and the South

b. Thirteenth Amendment

_____ 3. document that served as a promise to slaves that they would be free if the North won the war

c. Wade-Davis bill

_____ 4. a government pardon for an offense

d. Radical Republicans

_____ 5. place where John Wilkes Booth assassinated President Lincoln

e. President Johnson's plan

_____ 6. the amendment to the Constitution that officially abolished slavery in the United States

f. Ford's Theater

_____ 7. Reconstruction plan that restored property and political rights to most former Confederate leaders

g. amnesty

_____ 8. President who issued the Emancipation Proclamation in 1862

h. Abraham Lincoln

_____ 9. a group that spoke out strongly against Lincoln's plan for Reconstruction

i. Andrew Johnson

_____ 10. a series of laws that limited the rights of freed African Americans

j. black codes

Critical Thinking

Evaluate
Why did Radical Republicans oppose Reconstruction plans proposed by Abraham Lincoln and Andrew Johnson? Write your answer on a separate sheet of paper.

18 Section II. Conflicts Over Reconstruction

Complete each sentence on the lines below.

1. The law that Congress passed to limit President Johnson's power was the

_____.

2. During Reconstruction, the new southern governments reduced the power of

_____.

3. The process in which a U.S. President is accused of a crime is called

_____.

4. The _____ divided the South into five military regions and

placed an army general in charge of each region.

5. The _____ stated that states could not make laws that took

away any rights of citizens.

6. White Southerners who sided with the Republicans and the carpetbaggers were

called _____.

7. Republicans nominated _____ as their presidential candidate

in 1868.

8. To be readmitted to the Union, each state had to write a new state constitution

that supported voting rights for _____.

Critical Thinking

Evaluate
How did the Fourteenth Amendment define who was
a U.S. citizen? Explain your answer on a separate
sheet of paper.

Write *true* or *false* on the line below each sentence. If the sentence is false, rewrite it to make it true. Use a separate sheet of paper if you need more space.

1. Jim Crow laws were designed to achieve segregation by separating African Americans from white people in most public places.

   _____

2. Many white Southerners reacted to the changes brought about during Reconstruction by accepting the new laws.

   _____

3. Howard University helped find jobs and set up courts to ensure justice for emancipated African Americans.

   _____

4. The Compromise of 1877 named Rutherford Hayes as President and removed remaining federal troops from southern states.

   _____

5. The Fifteenth Amendment to the Constitution protected the right of African Americans to find long-lost family members.

   _____

6. Members of the Ku Klux Klan wanted to frighten African Americans and prevent them from voting.

   _____

Critical Thinking

Recognize Relationships
Why were most African Americans still unable to vote even after the Fifteenth Amendment was adopted? Write your answer on a separate sheet of paper.

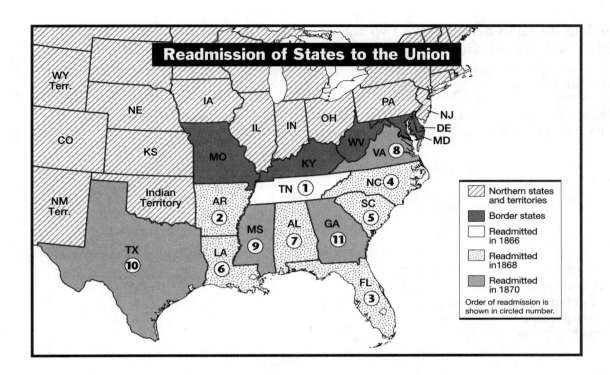

Readmission of States to the Union

Use the map to answer the following questions.

1. Which northern states are shown on the map?

_____

2. Which states were readmitted to the Union in 1870?

_____

3. Which state was readmitted to the Union in 1866?

_____

4. Which state was the last to be readmitted to the Union?

_____

5. Which states are border states?

_____

Complete the chart below. Write two details for each main idea. The first one is done for you.

Main Idea	Details
A. New railroads opened the West to settlement.	**1.** *The federal government helped pay for a transcontinental railroad.* **2.**
B. Texas cattle ranchers rounded up large herds of cattle and drove them north to "cow towns."	**3.** **4.**
C. Waves of people went west in search of gold or silver.	**5.** **6.**

Critical Thinking

Synthesize Information
You have decided to travel west to become a miner. Write a paragraph explaining where you plan to go and what you hope to do. Write your paragraph on a separate sheet of paper.

19 Section II. Farming on the Great Plains

Answer each question on the lines below.

1. What did the Homestead Act of 1862 offer to people?

_____

2. What was difficult about weather on the prairie?

_____

3. What did homesteaders do if they could not deal with the harshness of the prairie?

_____

4. How did cooperatives help farmers?

_____

5. Why did many farmers feel they were being treated unfairly by railroads?

_____

6. How did the Populists want income taxes to be changed?

_____

7. Why did farmers organize into groups known as Farmers' Alliances?

_____

8. What did the Interstate Commerce Commission do?

_____

Critical Thinking

Synthesize Information
Write a newspaper editorial encouraging farmers to join the Populist Party. Write your editorial on a separate sheet of paper.

Complete each sentence with a term from the box.

Geronimo	reservations	Wounded Knee
Dawes Act	Native American wars	Battle of Little Bighorn

1. The U.S. government passed the _____ in 1887 to break

up the reservations.

2. An attack by the Colorado militia on Native Americans gathered at Sand Creek

marked the beginning of the _____.

3. The government promised to give food, clothing, and supplies to Native

Americans if they would move to _____.

4. Native American warriors led by Sitting Bull and Crazy Horse defeated

Lieutenant Colonel George Custer in the _____.

5. The wars between Native Americans and settlers on the southern Great Plains

ended with the surrender of the Apache leader _____.

6. Native American resistance in the West ended after government troops killed

Sitting Bull and 200 Sioux people at _____.

Critical Thinking

Evaluate
What do you think of the reaction of government
troops to the Ghost Dance movement that came
to the Sioux reservation? Explain. Write your
answer on a separate sheet of paper.

Native American Lands

CANADA

Spokane   Blackfeet   Sioux   Chippewa
Yakima   L. Superior
          Nez Percé   Crow
Walla
Walla   Shoshone   Arapaho   L. Michigan
                              Shoshone   Sioux
Paiute   Ute

                         Navajo   Cherokee
                         Hopi   Cheyenne   Creek
              Mojave   Pueblo Arapaho   Choctaw
PACIFIC   Apache   Zuñi   Comanche   Seminole
OCEAN   Apache   Chickasaw

Land lost before 1850
Land lost 1850–1870
Land lost 1871–1890
Native American
reservations, 1890

0   250   500 mi
0   250   500 km

MEXICO

N
W   E
S

Gulf of Mexico

Use the map to answer the following questions.

1. Which three Native American reservations are closest to Mexico?

_____

2. Which four Native American reservations are closest to Canada?

_____

3. During which time period (after 1850) did Native Americans lose the least land?

_____

4. Describe where Native Americans lost the most land before 1850.

_____

Complete the chart below by listing inventions from the 1800s.
Write the name of each inventor and describe how each invention
changed American life. The first one is done for you.

Invention	Inventor	How the invention changed American life
Bessemer Process	Henry Bessemer	Stronger, less expensive steel helped make taller buildings, longer bridges, and more railroads.

Critical Thinking

Evaluate

What do you think the most important American invention of the 1800s was? Give at least two reasons for your answer. Write your answer on a separate sheet of paper.

20 Section II. Big Business and Labor Unions

Complete each sentence with a term from the box.

| American Federation of Labor | oil | strike | investment bankers |
| Standard Oil Company | Gilded Age | steel | |

1. The _____, led by Samuel Gompers, helped workers

   gain improvements in pay, hours, and working conditions.

2. At the end of the 1800s, the largest industries in the United States included

   the steel and _____ industries.

3. The early 1900s was called the _____ because widespread

   poverty was hidden by the great wealth of a few individuals.

4. One tool that unions used to force company owners to listen to their demands

   was the _____.

5. Andrew Carnegie was a powerful business owner who founded a

   _____ company just outside Pittsburgh.

6. Large corporations rely on _____ to organize the sale

   of stocks and provide loans.

7. John D. Rockefeller's _____ controlled more than

   90 percent of the country's oil refining.

Critical Thinking

Evaluate
Write a speech that a member of a labor union might
give to encourage others to join the union. Write your
speech on a separate sheet of paper.

Write the cause or effect of each sentence on the lines below.

1. Cause: _____

    Effect: The Chinese Exclusion Act is passed in 1882.

2. Cause: Many immigrants could not speak English very well.

    Effect: _____

3. Cause: _____

    Effect: Most new immigrants settled in port cities on the eastern coast.

4. Cause: _____

    Effect: Nativism was common in the late 1800s among many native-born Americans.

5. Cause: In the late 1800s, Cuba was trying to achieve independence from Spain.

    Effect: _____

6. Cause: _____

    Effect: Many immigrants lived in neighborhoods with people of the same ethnic background.

7. Cause: Most immigrants from northern and western Europe were Protestant and had some education and experience living under a representative government.

    Effect: _____

Critical Thinking

Draw Conclusions
Write an essay expressing your opinion about the Chinese Exclusion Act. Write your answer on a separate sheet of paper.

**Trends in Immigration,
1861–1880 and 1901–1920**

■ Northern and Western Europe
□ Southern and Eastern Europe
■ Other

24%
7%
69%
1861–1880

14%
13%
73%
1901–1920

Use the graphs to answer the following questions.

1. Between 1901 and 1920, which region had the lowest percentage of immigrants?

_____

2. Between 1861 and 1880, which region had the highest percentage of immigrants?

_____

3. How did immigration from southern and eastern Europe change between the two periods shown?

_____

_____

4. What conclusion can be made about the percentage of immigrants coming from northern and western Europe between 1861 and 1920?

_____

_____

Answer each question on the lines below.

1. What were two of the problems faced by cities at the beginning of the twentieth century?

   _____

2. Why did Jane Addams found Hull House?

   _____

3. Who was Boss William Marcy Tweed?

   _____

4. How did the Pendleton Civil Service Act affect employment in the government?

   _____

5. How did the Jim Crow laws affect African Americans?

   _____

6. What was the Supreme Court's ruling in *Plessy* v. *Ferguson*?

   _____

7. How did the Chinese Exclusion Act affect Chinese immigration to the United States?

   _____

8. How did the Interstate Commerce Act control interstate railroads?

   _____

Critical Thinking

Recognize Relationships
What were some of the positive and negative effects of the expansion of transportation and communication systems in the United States? Write your answer on a separate sheet of paper.

21 Section II. The Progressive Movement

Complete each sentence with a term from the box.

Niagara Movement	senators	alcohol	direct primary
Progressive	city-manager	muckraker	

1. Upton Sinclair was a _____ who described unclean conditions in factories that processed meat.

2. Women played an active role in getting Congress to pass the Eighteenth Amendment, which banned _____.

3. Some cities began to use a _____ system to handle the day-to-day activities of government.

4. A _____ is a person who believes in social progress through reform.

5. When the Seventeenth Amendment was passed, U.S. citizens gained the right to elect _____ directly.

6. The main goal of the _____ was to gain equality for African Americans.

7. After the _____ was adopted by some states, members of each political party voted to choose their candidates.

Critical Thinking

Evaluate
If you were a Progressive in the United States during the 1900s, which social problem would you choose to reform? Explain. Write your answer on a separate sheet of paper.

Choose the answer that best completes each of the following sentences. Circle the letter of the correct answer.

1. President Roosevelt used the Sherman Anti-Trust Act to
   a. form unions to protect the rights of workers.
   b. control the railroads that ran between states.
   c. break up large corporations that did not have any competition.
   d. control the meat-processing industry.

2. President Taft continued Roosevelt's policy of
   a. trustbusting.
   b. taxing the wealthy.
   c. reforming Congress.
   d. passing laws to help business.

3. President Wilson's New Freedom plan called for
   a. a government that worked to make social reforms.
   b. a smaller role for government.
   c. a foreign policy based on suffrage.
   d. a government that fought to end discrimination.

4. Teddy Roosevelt had some of his greatest accomplishments in
   a. the suffrage movement.
   b. the field of conservation.
   c. his work with labor unions.
   d. trustbusting.

5. The purpose of the Federal Reserve Act was to
   a. supervise banks using a system controlled by the government.
   b. monitor jails throughout the United States.
   c. create the Federal Bureau of Investigation.
   d. devise a plan to admit immigrants to the United States.

6. President Wilson passed the Adamson Act to
   a. prohibit child labor.
   b. create more large trusts that had no competition.
   c. help all Americans get a square deal.
   d. help interstate railway workers by limiting their workday to eight hours.

Critical Thinking

Evaluate
Do you think it is important for government to regulate business? Explain. Write your answer on a separate sheet of paper.

Women's Suffrage, 1919

AK 1913

WA 1910
OR 1912
ID 1896
MT 1914
ND
MN
VT NH ME
NY 1917
MA
RI

NV 1914
UT 1896
WY 1890
SD 1918
IA
WI
MI 1918
PA
CT
NJ
DE
MD

CA 1911
CO 1893
NE
IL
IN
OH
WV
VA

AZ 1912
NM
KS 1912
MO
KY
NC

OK 1918
AR
TN
SC

TX
LA
MS
AL
GA

HI

FL

█ Full suffrage (date effective)

In 1919, Alaska and Hawaii were U.S. territories with their own laws regarding women's suffrage. Both territories became states in 1959.

▨ Partial suffrage

▨ No suffrage

Use the map to answer the following questions.

1. Which was the only southwestern state that did not give women suffrage?

_____

2. Which part of the country had the most states that did not give women full suffrage or partial suffrage?

_____

3. Which was the only state on the east coast to give women full suffrage before 1919?

_____

4. How many states had partial suffrage for women?

_____

5. Which states gave women full suffrage in 1912?

_____

Section I. American Expansion in the Pacific

Answer each question on the lines below.

1. Why did some Americans believe that the United States should follow a policy of isolationism?

_____

2. Why did some Americans favor expansion?

_____

3. What did Commodore Matthew Perry do in Japan?

_____

4. Why did American business owners begin buying land in Hawaii?

_____

5. How did the United States take control of Hawaii?

_____

6. What was the Open Door policy?

_____

7. What agreement was reached in 1899 regarding the Samoan Islands?

_____

8. Why did the Boxers lead a rebellion in China in 1900?

_____

Critical Thinking

Evaluate
Do you think the United States had the right to control other countries? Explain. Write your answer on a separate sheet of paper.

A. Complete the cause/effect chart below about the Spanish-American War.

Cause	Effect
Many Americans blamed Spain for the explosion of the USS *Maine* on February 15, 1898.	**1.**
The United States and Spain signed a treaty officially ending the Spanish-American War.	**2.**
The Jones Act was passed in 1917.	**3.**

B. Answer each question on the lines below.

4. What did the United States force Cuba to do in 1901?

_____

5. What did Cuba become under the Teller Amendment?

_____

Critical Thinking

Synthesize Information
During the Spanish-American War, newspaper editors printed stories to get Americans to support the war. Do you think limits should be placed on what newspaper editors can print? Explain your answer on a separate sheet of paper.

Write *true* or *false* on the line below each sentence. If the sentence is false, rewrite it to make it true. Use a separate sheet of paper if you need more space.

1. President Theodore Roosevelt liked to use an old African saying, "Speak softly and carry a big stick."

   _____

2. Panama was part of El Salvador before the rebellion took place in 1903.

   _____

3. The new government of Panama agreed to give the United States land to build the Panama Canal in return for $10 million and $250,000 a year in rent.

   _____

4. George Goethals, an army doctor, led the effort to rid the canal zone of the deadly diseases yellow fever and malaria.

   _____

5. Dollar diplomacy was a follow-up to the Monroe Doctrine and a part of President Roosevelt's foreign policy.

   _____

6. President Woodrow Wilson intervened in Latin American countries when he thought guidance was needed.

   _____

7. President Woodrow Wilson sent troops to Mexico to capture Venustiano Carranza.

   _____

Critical Thinking

Evaluate
How did the Panama Canal help the United States become a world power? Write your answer on a separate sheet of paper.

The Spanish–American War, 1898

Use the map to answer the following questions.

1. Which cities are shown on the maps?

_____

2. Is Puerto Rico east or west of Cuba?

_____

3. To which city did the Spanish fleet sail?

_____

4. Which body of water did the U.S. Navy have to cross to reach Manila Bay?

_____

5. Where did the United States win battles?

_____

A. Number the events below in the order in which they occurred. The first one is done for you.

_____ **1.** German troops try to invade France.

___1___ **2.** Austrian Archduke Franz Ferdinand is assassinated.

_____ **3.** European countries declare war on each other.

_____ **4.** A German U-boat sinks the *Lusitania* without warning.

B. Complete the chart below by listing one advance in war technology on the ground, in the air, and at sea. Then, explain how each was used during the war.

Type of Warfare	Advance in Technology	How It Was Used
Land	**5.**	**6.**
Air	**7.**	**8.**
Sea	**9.**	**10.**

Critical Thinking

Make Inferences

If Archduke Franz Ferdinand had not been assassinated, would war still have broken out? Explain. Write your answer on a separate sheet of paper.

23 **Section II. The United States Enters the War**

Write *true* or *false* on the line below each sentence. If the sentence is false, rewrite it to make it true. Use a separate sheet of paper if you need more space.

1. In his re-election campaign, President Wilson argued that the United States should support the Allies in the war.

   _____

2. The United States moved closer to war when Japan sank five American ships in nine days.

   _____

3. President Wilson argued that the United States should enter the war to make the world "safe for democracy."

   _____

4. Communism is a theory in which the economy is controlled by the people.

   _____

5. The Selective Service Act asked men between the ages of 21 and 30 to volunteer to serve in the war.

   _____

6. Americans bought war bonds to help support the war effort.

   _____

7. Many African Americans moved north to find work in war industries and to escape the unfair treatment they faced in the South.

   _____

Critical Thinking

Synthesize Information
Write a short speech to Americans explaining why they should support the war. Write your speech on a separate sheet of paper.

Answer each question on the lines below.

1. Where was the first major battle that involved U.S. troops?

_____

2. What was life like for American soldiers in the trenches?

_____

3. Which battle marked the beginning of Germany's retreat?

_____

4. How did the United States aid in the war effort?

_____

5. What was the fourteenth point of President Wilson's peace plan?

_____

6. What was Germany required to pay and give up after the war?

_____

7. Why were some Republicans enemies of President Wilson?

_____

8. Why was President Wilson not able to fight for the League of Nations after his tour of the country?

_____

Critical Thinking

Synthesize Information
President Wilson proposed the League of Nations to prevent future wars. Write your own proposal to help prevent a war such as World War I from happening again. Write your proposal on a separate sheet of paper.

Europe During World War I

Map legend:
- Allied nations
- Central Powers
- Neutral nations
- Cities

NORWAY, SWEDEN, North Sea, Baltic Sea, DENMARK, RUSSIA, IRELAND, GREAT BRITAIN, NETH., BELG., GERMANY, LUX., ATLANTIC OCEAN, Paris, FRANCE, SWITZ., AUSTRIA-HUNGARY, SERBIA, MONTENEGRO, Sarajevo, ROMANIA, Caspian Sea, Black Sea, BULGARIA, PORTUGAL, SPAIN, Corsica (France), ITALY, OTTOMAN EMPIRE (TURKEY), PERSIA, MOROCCO (Spain), Sardinia (Italy), ALBANIA, GREECE, MOROCCO (France), ALGERIA (France), TUNISIA (France), Sicily (Italy), Mediterranean Sea, CYPRUS, ARABIA

Use the map to answer the following questions.

1. Were more countries members of the Central Powers or the Allied nations?

_____

2. Which was the largest country that was a member of the Allied nations?

_____

3. Which side had the best access to the Atlantic Ocean, the Allies or the Central Powers?

_____

4. Which cities are shown on the map?

_____

5. How far was Paris from the nearest Central Power?

_____

24 Section I. Business Booms

Complete each sentence on the lines below.

1. President _____ promised to return America to the life
   it had enjoyed before World War I.

2. Henry Ford made cars less expensive for American families by building them
   on an _____.

3. The _____ Scandal was the most famous scandal in the
   White House during Harding's presidency.

4. The _____ allowed people to pay for expensive items,
   such as appliances and furniture, over time.

5. One benefit of the _____ was that people did not have
   to shop for fresh produce as often.

6. Many companies gave their workers pension plans and paid vacations to keep
   them from joining _____.

7. The petroleum industry expanded as _____ became
   more popular.

8. It was the job of _____ to convince Americans that they
   needed more material goods.

Critical Thinking

Evaluate
Why might a company want people to purchase items
using an installment plan? Explain. Write your answer
on a separate sheet of paper.

Complete the chart below with names from the box. The first one is done for you.

Louis Armstrong	Langston Hughes	Gertrude Ederle	Babe Ruth
Duke Ellington	Nellie Tayloe Ross	Helen Wills	Zora Neale Hurston
Miriam Ferguson	F. Scott Fitzgerald	Jack Dempsey	Bessie Smith

Career	Famous People
Musician	*Louis Armstrong*
Writer	
Athlete	
Governor	

Critical Thinking

Evaluate
Write a radio news bulletin about Charles Lindbergh's flight across the Atlantic Ocean. Remember to answer the Five *Ws*: *who? what? where? when?* and *why?* Write your bulletin on a separate sheet of paper.

A. Match each item with its description. Write the correct letter on the line.

_____ 1. evangelist who built a large church in Los Angeles that appealed to people who had recently moved to the city

_____ 2. young teacher who taught Darwin's theory and was arrested and put in jail

_____ 3. a fixed number of a certain group of immigrants admitted to a country

_____ 4. to force someone to leave a country

_____ 5. a person who believes in a strict interpretation of the Bible or another religious book

_____ 6. Italian immigrants who were arrested in Massachusetts for a payroll robbery and the murder of a paymaster and his guard

_____ 7. a person who made or transported alcohol illegally

_____ 8. group that saw all foreigners as a threat to the United States

a. bootlegger

b. deport

c. Ku Klux Klan

d. fundamentalist

e. Aimee Semple McPherson

f. Nicola Sacco and Bartolomeo Vanzetti

g. John T. Scopes

h. quota

B. Number the events below in the order in which they occurred. The first one is done for you.

_____ 9. The Eighteenth Amendment is ratified.

_____ 10. Congress passes the National Origins Act.

_____ 11. Congress passes the Emergency Quota Act.

___1___ 12. Charles Darwin publishes his theory of evolution.

Critical Thinking

Evaluate
Do you agree or disagree with the government's decision to limit immigration? Explain. Write your answer on a separate sheet of paper.

U.S. Rural and Urban Populations, 1890–1920		
YEAR	PERCENTAGE RURAL	PERCENTAGE URBAN
1890	64.9	35.1
1900	60.4	39.6
1910	54.4	45.6
1920	48.8	51.2

Use the chart to answer the following questions.

1. What kinds of information are given in the chart?

_____

2. What percentage of people lived in rural areas in 1890?

_____

3. Did more people live in rural or urban areas in 1900?

_____

4. In which year did more people live in urban areas?

_____

5. Would you expect more people to live in rural or urban areas in 1930?

_____

Answer each question on the lines below.

1. What caused stock prices to fall in 1929?

_____

2. Why did the stock market crash on October 29, 1929?

_____

3. What were some of the signs of depression in the United States?

_____

4. What did the Federal Farm Board do?

_____

5. Why did President Hoover form the Reconstruction Finance Corporation?

_____

6. What did President Hoover do to overcome the Great Depression?

_____

7. What was the purpose of the Hawley-Smoot Tariff Act?

_____

8. What was the Dust Bowl?

_____

Critical Thinking

Evaluate
Do you agree or disagree with President Hoover's decision not to give surplus food and money to states? Explain. Write your answer on a separate sheet of paper.

25 Section II. Hard Times at Home

Write *true* or *false* on the line below each sentence. If the sentence is false, rewrite it to make it true. Use a separate sheet of paper if you need more space.

1. Franklin D. Roosevelt won the election of 1932 with strong support from African Americans and labor unions.

   _____

2. Mexican immigrants and Mexican Americans living in cities were paid high wages but had poor working conditions.

   _____

3. The Bonus Army said they would remain in Washington, D.C. until they received the land they had been promised.

   _____

4. A barrio is a community of Spanish-speaking people.

   _____

5. Tenant farmers were given land for free, but they had to give some of their crops to the government.

   _____

6. Franklin D. Roosevelt promised Americans a "New Deal."

   _____

Critical Thinking

Draw Conclusions
Why do you think segregation and discrimination against minorities increased during the Great Depression? Explain. Write your answer on a separate sheet of paper.

25 **Section III. The New Deal**

Complete the chart below by writing the purpose of each New Deal program. The first one is done for you.

Program	Purpose
Social Security Act	1. *to provide a pension to people over 65*
Wagner Act	2.
Federal Deposit Insurance Corporation	3.
Securities and Exchange Commission	4.
Tennessee Valley Authority	5.
Home Owners Loan Corporation	6.
Public Works Administration	7.

Critical Thinking

Synthesize Information
Explain two ways in which President Roosevelt's New Deal programs changed the United States. Write your answer on a separate sheet of paper.

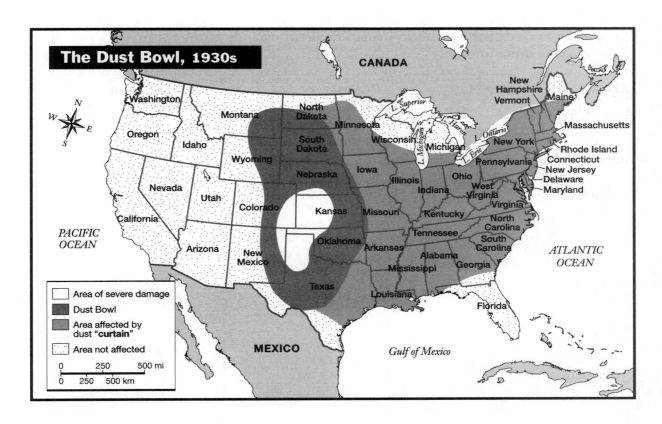

Use the map to answer the following questions.

1. How many states suffered severe damage from the effects of the Dust Bowl?

_____

2. Which part of the country was not affected by the Dust Bowl?

_____

3. Which state on the east coast was not affected by the dust "curtain"?

_____

4. How many miles did the Dust Bowl cover from its northern border to its southern border?

_____

Complete the chart below with information about each dictator. Some
of the chart is done for you.

Leader	Political Party	Country He Ruled	How He Came to Power
Adolf Hitler	*National Socialist Party, or Nazi Party*		
Benito Mussolini		*Italy*	
Joseph Stalin			*He seized control after Lenin's death.*

Critical Thinking

Make Inferences
Why do you think so many countries in Europe turned
to dictators following World War I? Explain. Write your
answer on a separate sheet of paper.

Choose the answer that best completes each of the following sentences. Circle the letter of the correct answer.

1. Early in the war, Germany

   a. stormed into western Europe by air and land.

   b. lost many battles and retreated to attack the Soviet Union.

   c. sided with Japan to take control of China.

   d. forced the Japanese to fight against the Allied forces in Asia.

2. The Soviet Union joined the Allies after

   a. France fell to the Germans.

   b. the United States entered the war.

   c. Germany led a surprise attack against it.

   d. Japan attacked its eastern border through China.

3. Roosevelt restricted exports to Japan to

   a. protest Japan's military expansion in Asia.

   b. keep Japan from attacking the east coast of the United States.

   c. help Japan invade countries in the Pacific.

   d. stop the Japanese from making an atomic bomb.

4. Congress declared war on Japan when

   a. Japan led a surprise raid of the Germans.

   b. Japanese bombers attacked the U.S. Pacific Fleet at Pearl Harbor.

   c. Japan invaded Poland.

   d. Paris, France, fell under a German invasion.

5. The first contribution that U.S. forces made to the war was to

   a. force Hitler to surrender.

   b. drop the atomic bomb on Japan.

   c. drive German troops out of North Africa.

   d. help the British force German troops out of London.

6. The massive attack against the Germans on the coast of Normandy was known as

   a. the Battle of Britain.

   b. the Battle of the Bulge.

   c. blitzkrieg.

   d. D-day.

Critical Thinking

Evaluate
Write a news report announcing the attack on Pearl Harbor. Remember to answer the Five *Ws*: *who?* *what? where? when?* and *why?* Use a separate sheet of paper for your report.

A. Match each cause on the left with its effect on the right. Write the correct letter on the line.

_____ **1.** The United States needs raw materials for the war.

_____ **2.** President Roosevelt becomes ill and dies in April 1945.

_____ **3.** Germany formally surrenders.

_____ **4.** Hitler adopts the "final solution" policy.

_____ **5.** Allies agree to form a world peace organization.

_____ **6.** Roosevelt and Churchill believe that all nations have the right to elect their own government.

_____ **7.** Japanese leaders refuse to surrender.

a. The United Nations is created to replace the League of Nations.

b. Harry S Truman becomes President of the United States.

c. The Atlantic Charter is signed.

d. The United States drops an atomic bomb on Hiroshima.

e. The war in Europe is over.

f. Thousands of people are killed each day in death camps.

g. Food supplies are rationed and people are encouraged to buy war bonds.

B. Answer each question on the lines below.

8. How did World War II help to end the Great Depression?

_____

9. Where did the key battle of the Pacific take place?

_____

Critical Thinking

Synthesize Information
You are a soldier who has just freed people in the concentration camp at Ohrdruf. Write a journal entry describing what you have seen and how you feel. Write your entry on a separate sheet of paper.

Casualties of World War II		
COUNTRY	**WOUNDED**	**TOTAL DEATHS**
China	1,752,951	2,200,000
France	400,000	563,000
Germany	5,000,000	4,200,000
Great Britain	277,077	357,000
Italy	66,000	395,000
Japan	4,000,000	1,972,000
Poland	236,606	5,798,178
United States	671,801	298,000
USSR	5,000,000	18,000,000

Total deaths are both civilian and military fatalities.
Wounded are military casualties only.

Use the chart to answer the following questions.

1. What information is shown in the chart?

_____

2. Which countries suffered losses in the millions?

_____

3. Which two countries had the most soldiers wounded during World War II?

_____

4. Which country suffered the fewest deaths during World War II?

_____

Write *true* or *false* on the line below each sentence. If the sentence is false, rewrite it to make it true. Use a separate sheet of paper if you need more space.

1. As part of the Yalta agreement, all of Germany was given to the Soviet Union.

_____

2. The iron curtain separated Soviet-controlled nations from the rest of Europe.

_____

3. The alliance known as NATO included the United States, Canada, and the countries of Asia.

_____

4. In response to NATO, the Soviet Union organized a military alliance with its Eastern European satellites known as the Warsaw Pact.

_____

5. After the Communist takeover in China, the Nationalists fled to the Philippine Islands, where they formed their own government.

_____

6. Many Jewish survivors of the Holocaust moved to Palestine after World War II.

_____

7. A crisis began in the Middle East when Gamal Abdel Nasser took control of the Panama Canal.

_____

Critical Thinking

Draw Conclusions
Why do you think the United States was against the spread of communism after World War II? What dangers concerned Americans? Write your answer on a separate sheet of paper.

27 Section II. The Korean War and the Red Scare

Answer each question on the lines below.

1. Why did many liberal Democrats abandon President Truman in the 1948 election?

_____

2. How was Korea divided after World War II?

_____

3. What caused the start of the Korean War?

_____

4. Why did the United States refer to its involvement in the Korean War
   as a "police action"?

_____

5. Why did President Truman fire General Douglas MacArthur?

_____

6. What is a demilitarized zone?

_____

7. What were Julius and Ethel Rosenberg accused of doing?

_____

8. What led to the downfall of Joseph McCarthy?

_____

Critical Thinking

Evaluate
In what way did the actions of Joseph McCarthy
violate people's civil rights? Explain. Write your
answer on a separate sheet of paper.

Complete the chart below to show major domestic and foreign events during the Eisenhower administration. The first one is done for you.

Domestic	Foreign
1. *passage of the Federal Aid Highway Act*	5.
2.	6.
3.	7.
4.	8.

Critical Thinking

Make Inferences
Why do you think efforts to create a test-ban treaty to stop the testing of nuclear weapons were unsuccessful? Explain. Write your answer on a separate sheet of paper.

27 Section IV. Life in the Fifties

Complete each sentence on the lines below.

1. During the 1950s, many people moved to _____ on the outskirts of most American cities.

2. The increase in population after World War II became known as the _____.

3. The first planned community, called _____, was built on Long Island, New York.

4. The increasing influence of _____ meant that families spent less time reading, listening to the radio, or talking about the day's events.

5. Elvis Presley was the first national _____ star.

6. The difference between teens and their parents was known as the _____.

7. Young people who grew up in the 1950s are often called the first _____.

8. By the end of the 1950s, _____ held one third of all jobs.

9. The Dodgers broke the racial barrier in baseball by signing _____ to a contract.

Critical Thinking

Evaluate
Do you think there is a generation gap today between the nation's younger and older generations? Write a journal entry describing your thoughts. Write your entry on a separate sheet of paper.

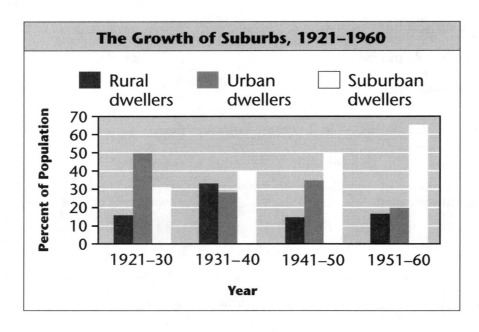

The Growth of Suburbs, 1921–1960

Use the graph to answer the following questions.

1. What does the graph show?

_____

2. During which years did most Americans live in urban areas?

_____

3. During which years did the number of rural, urban, and suburban dwellers come closest to being equal?

_____

4. Where did the largest group of Americans live from 1941 to 1950?

_____

5. What trend do you see reflected in the graph?

_____

Complete the chart by answering the questions *Who? Where? When?* and *Why?* for the two events listed below.

Who?		
What?	Bay of Pigs Invasion	Building of the Berlin Wall
Where?		
When?		
Why?		

Critical Thinking

Evaluate
Do you think that the United States should have been involved in the invasion of Cuba? Explain. Write your answer on a separate sheet of paper.

Complete the chart below by filling in names of Supreme Court
cases that were important during the Kennedy administration.
Then, summarize the decision of the Supreme Court in each case.
The first one is done for you.

Supreme Court Case	Supreme Court Ruling
A. *Engel* v. *Vitale*	1. *School officials cannot force students to pray.* 2.
B.	3. 4.
C.	5. 6.

Critical Thinking

Synthesize Information
You are a Peace Corps volunteer who has been
working to help people in developing countries for
the past two years. Write a letter to a friend back
home describing what you have been doing. Write
your letter on a separate sheet of paper.

Complete the chart by writing two facts about each of the civil rights protests listed below. The first fact is done for you.

Protest	Facts
Greensboro, North Carolina	1. *The protesters were nonviolent and remained seated.* 2.
Freedom Ride	3. 4.
Birmingham, Alabama	5. 6.
March on Washington	7. 8.

Critical Thinking

Synthesize Information
You are a reporter at the March on Washington. Write a newspaper article about the event on a separate sheet of paper.

Federal Funding for the U.S. Space Program, 1950–1965

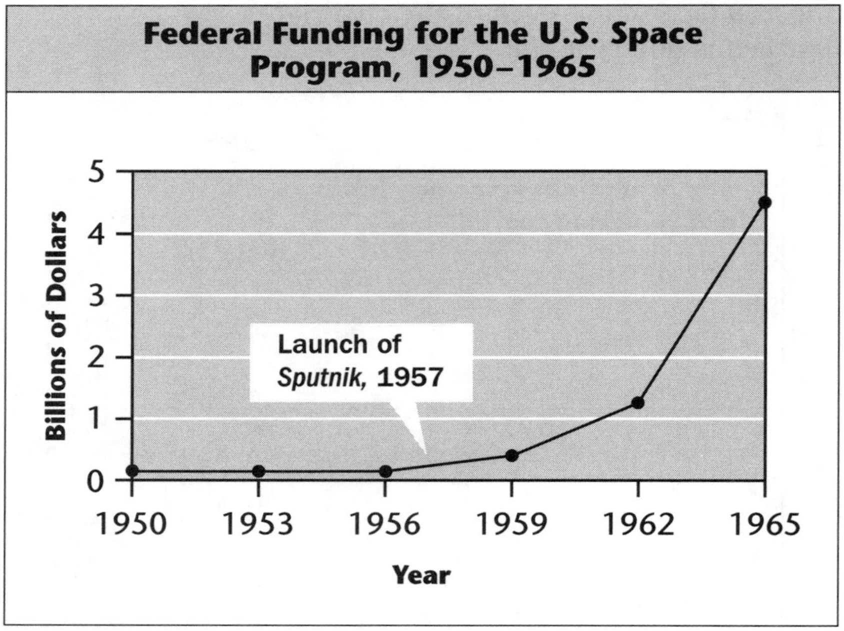

Use the graph to answer the following questions.

1. What does the graph show?

_____

2. Did funding increase or decrease after the launch of *Sputnik* in 1957?

_____

3. How much money did the federal government give to the space program in 1962?

_____

4. For how many years does the graph give information?

_____

5. What trend do you see reflected in the graph?

_____

29 Section I. The Great Society

Complete the chart below by writing the goals and improvements of each Great Society program. The first one is done for you.

Program	Goals and Improvements
Project Head Start	*Helps prepare children from low-income families for elementary school*
Department of Housing and Urban Development	
Wilderness Preservation Act	
Elementary and Secondary Education Act	
Higher Education Act	
National Foundation on the Arts and the Humanities	
Medicare	

Critical Thinking

Evaluate
Write a speech supporting President Johnson's Great Society. Give two reasons why Great Society programs are good for all Americans. Write your speech on a separate sheet of paper.

A. Number the events below in the order in which they occurred. The first one is done for you.

_____ **1.** President Johnson appoints the Kerner Commission to study race riots.

_____ **2.** The Voting Rights Act is passed by Congress.

_____ **3.** Martin Luther King Jr. is assassinated in Memphis, Tennessee.

_____ **4.** The Black Panther Party is formed in California.

___1___ **5.** Congress passes the Civil Rights Act.

B. Choose the answer that best completes each of the following sentences. Circle the letter of the correct answer.

6. The Civil Rights Act

   a. created separate schools for African Americans.

   b. required that all racial groups receive equal pay.

   c. gave women the right to vote.

   d. outlawed segregation in public places.

7. Unlike Martin Luther King Jr., Malcolm X believed in

   a. equal rights for African Americans.

   b. using violence to gain rights for African Americans.

   c. overthrowing the United States government.

   d. rights for African American women.

8. Betty Friedan's book, _The Feminine Mystique_, led to

   a. a revival of feminism.

   b. rioting around the country.

   c. the passage of the Equal Rights Amendment.

   d. the end of discrimination in the United States.

9. Many Native Americans blamed their poor living conditions on

   a. the American Indian Movement.

   b. the federal government.

   c. poor weather.

   d. the Black Panthers.

Critical Thinking

Evaluate

Do you think women and minorities enjoy equal rights today? Write a newspaper editorial explaining your views. Write your editorial on a separate sheet of paper.

Section III. Conflict in Vietnam

Answer each question on the lines below.

1. Who were the Viet Cong?

_____

2. Why was Ngo Dinh Diem such an unpopular ruler?

_____

3. What events led to the passage of the Gulf of Tonkin Resolution?

_____

4. What was Operation Rolling Thunder?

_____

5. What problems did American troops face while fighting in Vietnam?

_____

6. What groups of Americans were most affected by the draft?

_____

7. What steps did some young Americans take to avoid going to war?

_____

8. Why was the Tet Offensive a turning point in the war?

_____

Critical Thinking

Synthesize Information
Create a timeline of at least four events leading up
to and occurring during the Vietnam War. Draw your
timeline on a separate sheet of paper.

Federal Funding for Public Schools, 1960–1968

Use the graph to answer the following questions.

1. During which years was federal funding less than $1 billion?

_____

2. During which year was federal funding over $2.5 billion?

_____

3. If federal funding increased at approximately the same rate as it did between 1966 and 1968, what would federal funding be in 1970?

_____

4. During which years did federal funding increase the least?

_____

Write *true* or *false* on the line below each sentence. If the sentence is false, rewrite it to make it true. Use a separate sheet of paper if you need more space.

1. The My Lai massacre was committed by North Vietnamese soldiers.

   _____

2. Some of the students killed at Kent State University in 1970 were not participating in the antiwar protest.

   _____

3. On April 30, 1975, the United States decided to withdraw troops from Saigon.

   _____

4. Eugene McCarthy and Robert Kennedy were Democrats who strongly opposed U.S. involvement in Vietnam.

   _____

5. The Ho Chi Minh Trail was a supply route used by the North Vietnamese to send supplies to troops in the South.

   _____

6. As a result of the 1973 truce, the United States stopped all bombing in the war.

   _____

7. Henry Kissinger began secret talks with North Vietnamese leaders.

   _____

Critical Thinking

Evaluate
What were some of the negative effects of the truce that was signed in 1973? Do you think the truce improved the situation or made it worse? Write your answer on a separate sheet of paper.

Complete each sentence with a term from the box.

Environmental Protection Agency	Supreme Court
Democratic National Committee	Communist countries
House Un-American Activities Committee	affirmative action

1. The _____ investigated charges of Communist

activity among Americans during the 1940s and 1950s.

2. In 1971, the _____ ruled that school districts must

bus children to schools away from their neighborhoods.

3. The Watergate scandal began when five men were arrested for breaking into

the offices of the _____ .

4. During Nixon's administration, a bill was signed that created the

_____ to enforce environmental laws.

5. During his presidency, Nixon worked to improve relations with

_____ such as the Soviet Union and the People's

Republic of China.

6. President Nixon supported _____ programs to increase

opportunities for African Americans, women, Latinos, and Native Americans.

Critical Thinking

Make Inferences
Richard Nixon chose to resign as President rather than
face an impeachment trial in Congress. Why do you
think Nixon made this choice? Explain your answer on
a separate sheet of paper.

30 Section III. Domestic Crises

Complete the chart below. Write who was President at the time of each event. Then, write a description of each event. Finally, write the outcome of each event. The first one is done for you.

Event	President	Description	Outcome
WIN Program	Ford	Ford's plan to reduce inflation by cutting spending.	Americans did not take the program seriously.
Nixon Pardoned			
Three Mile Island Accident			
Camp David Accords			
Iran Hostage Crisis			

Critical Thinking

Draw Conclusions
Americans were divided over President Ford's decision to pardon Richard Nixon. Do you agree or disagree with Ford's decision? Do you think his actions caused him to lose the election of 1976? Write your answers on a separate sheet of paper.

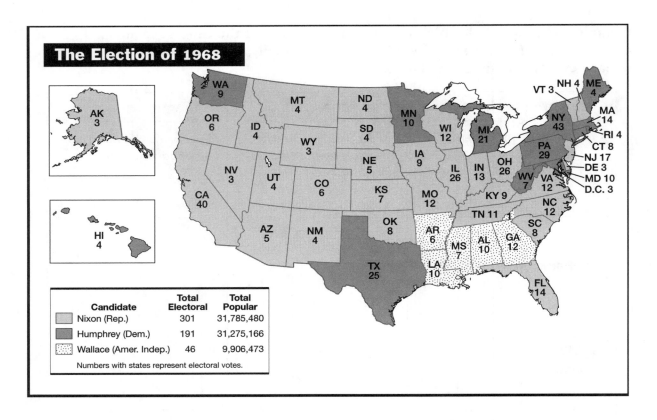

The Election of 1968

Candidate	Total Electoral	Total Popular
Nixon (Rep.)	301	31,785,480
Humphrey (Dem.)	191	31,275,166
Wallace (Amer. Indep.)	46	9,906,473

Numbers with states represent electoral votes.

Use the map to answer the following questions.

1. How many states did Wallace win in the 1968 election?

_____

2. Which state gave Nixon the most electoral votes?

_____

3. What is the lowest number of electoral votes held by any state or states?

_____

4. Which candidate won Wisconsin's electoral votes in the 1968 election?

_____

Choose the answer that best completes each of the following sentences. Circle the letter of the correct answer.

1. The Moral Majority was

   a. a part of Congress responsible for social issues.

   b. a group of conservative justices on the Supreme Court.

   c. a conservative group that promoted "family values."

   d. a group of reporters who wrote about religious issues.

2. The Iran-Contra hearings were held by Congress to

   a. learn who was responsible for the sale of weapons to Iran.

   b. examine the effect of the Cold War on the Iranians.

   c. investigate trade relations between Iran and Nicaragua.

   d. question rebels from the Soviet Union.

3. President Reagan extended his conservative policies by reshaping

   a. the banks.

   b. the House of Representatives.

   c. Congress.

   d. the Supreme Court.

4. President Reagan believed that

   a. reducing tax rates would help the economy.

   b. the federal government was too big.

   c. there should be less federal spending on the environment.

   d. all of the above

5. The federal deficit increased during Reagan's presidency because he

   a. allowed Congress to spend too much money on education.

   b. spent a great deal of money on the military.

   c. loaned large amounts of money to poor democratic nations.

   d. increased spending on social programs for the poor.

6. President Reagan believed that through deregulation

   a. companies would be forced to institute energy-saving practices.

   b. factories would be required to reduce air pollution from smokestacks.

   c. the economy would slow down.

   d. businesses would become more profitable.

Critical Thinking

Evaluate

What type of role do you think the government should play in people's lives? Explain. Write your answer on a separate sheet of paper.

Complete each sentence with a term from the box.

Operation Desert Storm	Clean Air Act	Panama
Americans With Disabilities Act	Berlin Wall	apartheid
Tiananmen Square		

1. President Bush supported the _____, which opened up the workplace to millions of Americans who would not otherwise be able to work.

2. The amendments to the _____ focused on acid rain, smog, and hazardous pollutants from cars and other vehicles.

3. After several hundred protesters were killed in _____, President Bush stopped the sale of military supplies to China.

4. President Bush sent U.S. troops to capture Manuel Noriega, the ruler of _____, who was involved in international drug trading.

5. On January 16, 1991, the United States and its allies launched an attack on Iraq called _____.

6. In 1989, communism began to collapse in Eastern Europe when the _____ was opened.

7. After more than 50 years of racial segregation, South Africa final began to change its policy of _____.

Critical Thinking

Evaluate
Thousands of young people celebrated when the Berlin Wall was opened. Why do you think young people were joyful when this happened? Write your answer on a separate sheet of paper.

Write *true* or *false* on the line below each sentence. If the sentence is false, rewrite it to make it true. Use a separate sheet of paper if you need more space.

1. President Clinton's main foreign policy strategy was to contain communism.

_____

2. President Clinton sent U.S. troops to Rwanda, Africa, to help make sure shipments of food and medicine were being delivered to the people.

_____

3. In October 2000, the Navy destroyer USS *Cole* was attacked while refueling in Yemen.

_____

4. President Clinton was impeached, but found not guilty, for lying to a grand jury and obstructing justice.

_____

5. In the election of 2000, Albert Gore Jr. ran against George W. Bush.

_____

6. Operation Enduring Freedom began when the United States dropped bombs on targets in Kenya, Africa.

_____

7. The Director of Homeland Security was a new Cabinet-level position established to coordinate efforts to make Americans safe at home.

_____

Critical Thinking

Evaluate
Create a timeline using the dates in Section III. Label each date with an event that happened at that time. Draw your timeline on a separate sheet of paper.

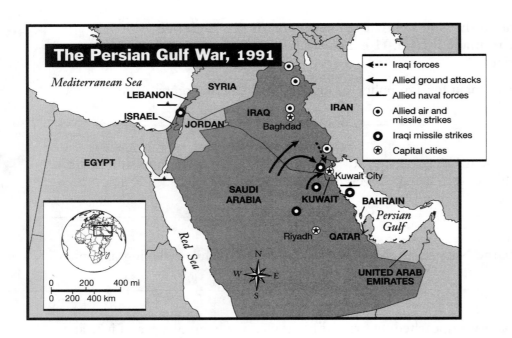

Use the map to answer the following questions.

1. What is the capital of Iraq?

_____

2. What body of water would Iraq gain access to by taking control of Kuwait?

_____

3. Approximately how many miles is Kuwait City from Baghdad?

_____

4. Name the two countries that share Saudi Arabia's northern border.

_____

5. What body of water is between Saudi Arabia and Egypt?

_____

Write *true* or *false* on the line below each sentence. If the sentence is false, rewrite it to make it true. Use a separate sheet of paper if you need more space.

1. One of the earliest models of a workable computer came in 1946 and was called SALT.

   _____

2. The World Wide Web was introduced in 1991 and contains all the documents on the Internet.

   _____

3. In 1998, the United States began working with other countries to build the Hubble Space Telescope.

   _____

4. Every cell in the human body is made up of genes that are passed on from parent to child.

   _____

5. Genetic engineering is impacting agriculture by allowing scientists to reproduce farmland indoors.

   _____

6. Most telephones, televisions, VCRs, CD players, and other everyday items use computer technology.

   _____

Critical Thinking

Evaluate
How have computers changed your life? Explain.
Write your answer on a separate sheet of paper.

Answer each question on the lines below.

1. Why did President George W. Bush propose federal tax cuts?

_____

2. How did GATT try to increase global trade?

_____

3. Why does the number of jobs in the healthcare field continue to grow?

_____

4. How do today's U.S. immigrants differ from those in the early part of the twentieth century?

_____

5. Why is the number of manufacturing jobs in the United States declining?

_____

6. For what reasons do people support bilingual education?

_____

7. How do some states address the healthcare needs of low-income families?

_____

8. How do planned senior communities serve the elderly population?

_____

Critical Thinking

Evaluate
You have just been elected President of the United States. Which issue would you make your first priority? Explain your decision on a separate sheet of paper.

A. Match each item with its description. Write the correct letter on the line.

_____ **1.** a thin layer of gas that shields Earth against harmful radiation from the Sun

a. carbon dioxide

_____ **2.** the rise in the average temperature of Earth over time

b. Kyoto Protocol

_____ **3.** organization that works to help people achieve a decent level of health

c. global warming

_____ **4.** a gas that occurs naturally in the air

d. ozone layer

_____ **5.** treaty that was written to try to slow global warming

e. World Health Organization

B. Complete the chart below with some of the problems the United States faces and their solutions.

Problem	Solutions
Global Warming	6.
Global Diseases	7.

Critical Thinking

Synthesize Information
What are ways you can conserve energy in your daily life? Explain your answer on a separate sheet of paper.

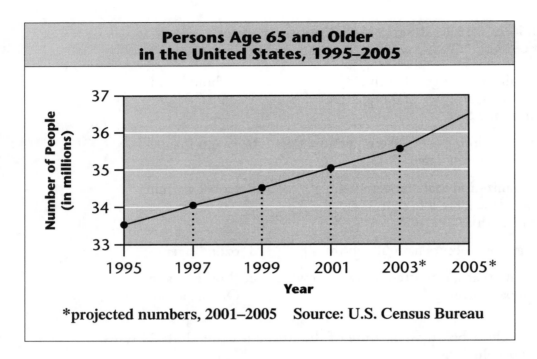

**Persons Age 65 and Older
in the United States, 1995–2005**

*projected numbers, 2001–2005   Source: U.S. Census Bureau

Use the graph to answer the following questions.

1. What information does the graph show?

_____

2. How many people age 65 and older were in the United States in 1997?

_____

3. How many people age 65 and older were in the United States in 2001?

_____

4. By how much did the number of people age 65 and older increase
between 1997 and 1999?

_____

5. Based on the information in the graph, do you think that the number of
people age 65 and older will increase or decrease in the year 2010?

_____